His Winnowing Fan

And Other Unpreached Sermons

S. H. Shepherd

Contents

"The harvest truly is plentiful, but the laborers are few. Therefore pray the Lord of the harvest to send out laborers into His harvest."
– Matt. 9:37-38.

Preface

Many ministers and pastors of every denomination and parish believe that most people are not amenable, or receptive, to hearing many of the messages of the Bible, including many of the messages that Jesus gave to the world. They believe them to be too harsh for most people to hear or that their preaching would cause too much controversy and so drive many members as well as newcomers away. Therefore, nearly every sermon preached from church or missionary pulpit is decidedly of the tamer, more acceptable type, such as Jesus's teachings on love, mercy, forgiveness and compassion. However, His other teachings, the unpreached,[1] or seldom if ever preached ones hold the key to our deliverance from many if not all of the problems we face daily in the world as individuals, communities and nations.

It is particularly true of the teachings that have to do with eschatology. Billy Graham called the reality of hell one of the hardest of all teachings of Christianity to receive.

I recently read an article written by Jerome R. Dollard, O.S.B, published in 1982, with the heading, "The Kingdom of God." It states: "It would be appropriate to say that the church's department of eschatology is temporarily closed." It is my opinion that, worldwide, it remains closed.

We needn't fear the Word of God, for it teaches what is true, and Biblical truth should never be feared, no matter how uncomfort-able it may be to hear, because truth makes us realize what is wrong and should be changed in our lives (2 Tim. 3:16-17). The messages that concern God's judgement and man's eternal future

---

[1] Unpreached versus those that are recanted for heretical reasons.

5

should be preached more often, for they keep us on our toes, alert us to be more watchful of what we say and do, and help us act more naturally with honesty, integrity and truthfulness. In addition, important aspects of Christian life are seldom if ever taught in church or elsewhere, such as how evil should be treated – should it be tolerated or opposed, and how should Christians view the tolerant world?

It is important to remember that God's Spirit is more than a spirit of love, mercy, forgiveness and compassion. It is also a Spirit of truth, austerity, righteousness and judgment.

Another reason we do not hear the full teachings of Jesus is because it raises many questions about Christian theology and eschatology that many Christians and non-Christians alike do not have adequate answers for, such as: Why do we have to suffer and die? Why does God allow evil to exist in the world? Do heaven and hell really exist? What is man's purpose for living? What is proper Christian conduct in the world? These questions and more are answered in this book.

Whether people want to hear about God's truth, sovereignty, judgment and righteousness or not, the unpreached messages described in this book are crucial for our day and age, and should be heard not just once a year on Sunday, but throughout the year, and from all preaching platforms. We need to keep them in mind because they can seriously affect the way that we live.

The parable of the *Ten Minas* testifies that God is a great King, one who is fair to those He favors by giving them resources in which to steward, but who executes severe punishment on His enemies.

Each chapter of this book discusses an important topic that is seldom if ever elucidated from home or missionary pulpit, but from which many sermons could be preached. They tell us that the purposes of God are not the purposes of man, that God's purposes transcend man's, and also man, himself. The book, for some, will be an awakening, a sprinkling of holy water, a new experience. For others, it will be a journey through the Scriptures, a revisitation of what the Bible says about us and the great King.

As exemplified by His teachings and miracles, Jesus has the righteousness, power, certitude and decisiveness of God as well as His love, mercy and compassion. His authority over both heaven and earth (Matt. 28:18) testify of these things, as do His many works of power and mercy. If only one side of Him is preached, we lose the other, and if we are seldom if ever reminded of the other, we quickly lose our way.

How we view the afterlife determines in large part how we view ourselves and the world. It affects the quality of life. It plays a big role in how we conduct ourselves, how we manage our time and treat others. Perhaps there is nothing more important for a person to understand than they are accountable to God for life and for what they say and do. The Word of God condemns serving self and public opinion. While rightly dividing the word of truth (2 Tim. 2:15), we are to be guided and directed by it, but that is not what we are seeing.

The fear of God is not being preached or otherwise taught today. It has gone out of style. We hear only of God's love and compassion, the part of the Gospel that is most receptive to the majority. But God is very much to be feared, and fear of Him is what He expects of each of us, Christian and non-Christian alike.

Chapter 1 His Winnowing Fan

"His winnowing fan is in His hand, and He will thoroughly clean out His threshing floor, and gather the wheat into His barn; but the chaff He will burn with unquenchable fire." - Luke 3:17 (NKJV).

This verse, spoken by John the Baptist, is one of the seldom preached messages of Jesus Christ. This assessment is based on many published sermons of past and present famous Bible scholars, teachers and theologians. However, it is one of the most riveting and spiritually awakening of all the messages in the Bible. It deserves our attention, and should be preached more often, for no passage of Scripture is more full of meaning for us today than the passage of the winnowing fan.

Some believe the threshing floor is the church, which includes all believers, but when the passage is compared to similar verses of the Bible, such as Ps. 91:3, Eccl. 12:14, Dan. 7:9, Matt. 3:13, John 15:6, and 2 Cor. 5:10, it is obvious that it takes in all of humanity, and therefore applies to all people. It speaks of the weeding out process that is going to occur on that fateful day called the Day of Judgment.

The chaff will burn with unquenchable fire, which portends a fate of severe suffering.

The poignant phrase had no misunderstanding for those who heard it when Jesus walked the earth, for almost all people then lived off the land planting seeds and reaping harvests, which included the wheat harvest, and even now the phrase is easy to understand, although many people are no longer familiar with planting and harvesting.

Its meaning is further made apparent in the parable of the *Wheat and the Tares* (Matthew 13:24-30 and 36-43), where the kingdom of heaven is compared to a man who sowed good seed in his field. but while he slept, his enemy came and sowed tares among the wheat. When the grain sprouted, the tares also sprouted. When his servants asked him if he wanted them to go and gather up the tares, he told them no, for then they would also gather up some of the wheat, but to wait until harvest time and then separate the two, one to be stored in the barn and the other to be destroyed by fire. In the parable's explanation (verses 36-43), Jesus told his disciples that He was the sower of the good seed and the devil was the sower of the tares.

It tells us that there is a difference between good and evil, here and now, and, as well will see, it is high time that it is recognized. It tells us that a reward awaits the righteous, but punishment the wicked. It tells us that death is not the end, which in effect tells us that the soul lives on in one of two eternal states, or destinations.

St. Matthew expresses it this way:

"And even now the ax is laid to the root of the trees. Therefore, every tree which does not bear good fruit is cut down and thrown into the fire." - Matt. 3:10.

The tree is not merely to be trimmed, but cut down, signifying final, unchangeable resolution and judgement.

The ax is already laid at the root of the trees. It speaks of impending judgment, the imminent and ever-present peril, the divine vengeance that awaits us all, and it is not something that will be delayed any longer. Effectively, it is the judgment that will be will be passed on everyone who has ever lived. It is a beacon of warning alerting us of the importance of recognizing our

9

responsibility to God, and it unmistakenly informs us that our pride and vanity and ignorance must be dealt with now, at this time.

The passage In its entirety is a striking figure of speech, a distinct message of the threatening wrath that is to come on whoever is not counted worthy of heaven. It tells us that Jesus is the Judge and it is He who will garner into his barn those who will live in heaven but bind those who will be burned with unquenchable fire. It is not something that the world wants to hear, but it is something that the world needs to hear.

Highly does it become us to speak of Christ and humbly of ourselves, for John the Baptist and Jesus both tell us that it is through Christ and Christ alone that God intends that His kingdom of peace and justice be established.

Many people are ignorant of God's Word and its relevance to them. Not only are people reading much less today, but fewer ever read the Word of God and find out for themselves what it says. Add to this sad state of affairs the great conformity that has dropped over this country and the world due to education by popular media and the regimentation of social life, and the result is an ignorance of God and His purposes for humanity in the eyes of many people.

"My people are destroyed for lack of knowledge." - Hos. 4:6.

No longer are we hearing about the eternal fate that hangs over every head like the sword of Damocles. No longer are we being warned about a place called hell. The result is a moral landslide in this country and in the world that may never be reversed.

Winston Churchill said, "The moral landslide in Great Britain can be traced to the fact that heaven and hell are no longer proclaimed throughout the land."

When people have no fear of the judgement and the afterlife confronting them, they are unable to see further than the horizons of this world. When they're made aware of it, however, the brevity of life becomes apparent to them. Then they begin to realize that nothing lasts forever and that time and what they do with it is extremely important.

When we know of imminent danger, we have a chance of avoiding it. If messages like the winnowing fan are never or seldom preached, then people can go blindly through life as though that is all there is, and end up facing certain destruction in the end.

"And I will winnow them with a winnowing fan...since they do not return from their ways." - Jer. 15:7.

When we understand that God requires an account of the way we live, it changes how we live. As mentioned previously, it makes us more watchful of what we say and do, and helps us to act more naturally with honesty, integrity and truthfulness.

Those who hear and acknowledge the truth about the Word of God have an eternal perspective that gives them new hope, hope that is needed for today and the future. It helps them get through the many problems and frustrations of life. It changes their outlook on the world and on others. They begin to see a difference between the vainglorious fleeting pursuits and accomplishments of this world, which have only temporal significance, and little or no significance compared with life everlasting, and what is of value and importance to God that have everlasting significance.

The handwriting is on the wall, but no one will proclaim it.

Chapter 2 The Suffering of Man, Is it Fair?

During suffering or when others suffer, we may wonder why God permits it. Why does He allow calamities, such as hurricanes and tornadoes, as well as sickness, disease and wars to devastate the population when He could easily prevent them from occurring?

Since the Fall (Genesis 3), suffering has been an inescapable part of the human condition. In the 19th and early 20th Centuries, in this country alone, there were scourges of diseases, including small pox, malaria, yellow fever and polio that took millions of lives.[2][3] The influenza pandemic of 1918-1919 killed between 20 and 40 million people.[4][5]

Everyone is familiar in some way with the ill treatment of human beings during times of war, but also in times of peace, when lives have been lost, displaced and forever altered – men, women, children and families ripped apart as the world bears witness to the ongoing invasion of evil.

Many in the South In this country grimly remember to this day General Sherman's march to Atlanta and the eastern seaboard during the Civil War, when barbarous blue-uniformed hoards ravaged and plundered, causing untold thousands to suffer and die from cruel and unjust treatment, depriving them of the necessities of life.[6] And many in the North whose fore-fathers fought in the war still remember the cruel treatment of captured

---

[2] htpps://www. cdc.gov. malaria > about > history.

[3] Malaria wasn't considered eliminated in the US until 1951 through the use of insecticides, drainage ditches and window screens.

[4] https://virus.stanford.edu/uda/.

[5] Exceeds several times the death toll of the 2019-2022 COVID pandemic.

[6] Edward Achorn, Every Drop of Blood.

Union troops in Southern internment camps, like Andersonville. Scars caused by such ill treatment last for many years.

"Never can true reconciliation grow where wounds of deadly hate have pierced so deep." - John Milton, *Paradise Lost*,

The Russian Revolution, which materialized at the end of WWI, was based on the dogmatic, atheist philosophy of Marxism that led to the century-long perpetuation of Soviet Communism under Joseph Stalin. The response by Germany led to the dictatorial rule of Adolf Hitler. Both totalitarian regimes caused untold human suffering on a scale never before seen, including the great man-made famine in Ukraine during the 1930s and the relentless persecution of the Jewish people and others of Eastern Europe. It brought destruction to Germany had a devastating effect on millions and millions of people, including Christians and those of other religions, abducting them to slave camps, mines and prisons, torturing and depriving them not only of their potential contributions to society, but forcing them to live in squalor and agony for years.

"In our day immeasurable suffering has been afflicted upon numerable persons because we live in a very terrible time. Not only have millions and millions of persons died by violence, but millions of persons have been displaced, torn out of their houses and their homes and sent somewhere else. It's a world which is almost immeasurable in the amount of suffering that it has endured. In just a few years we had two world wars that slaughtered millions and millions of people and disrupted the life of the whole planet." - Archibald MacLeish, *The Dialogues of Archibald MacLeish and Mark Van Doren*.

Countless tales came out of WWII, the Korean War and the

Vietnam war that illustrate the tragedy of meaningless suffering, which is an outcome of war. For example, there were instances during the Battle of Britain where families that had been bombed out in one location had gone to live in another location, only to be bombed out again, and each time their numbers diminished.[7]

These things make a sort of pattern of meaninglessness. They make people have to deal with unresolvable, meaningless suffering. Many turn away from God, and end up blaming Him for the tragedy, for what other reason could there be?

Habakkuk asked God during a time of terrible trouble in Israel, "Why do you idly look at traitors and remain silent when the wicked swallows up the man more righteous than he?" - Hab. 1:13.

"Why do You cast me off? Why do I go mourning because of the oppression of the enemy?" - Ps. 43:2.

We need but look to the Bible to learn about Job, who is the symbol of undeserved, meaningless suffering, having endured a suffering that no one can understand. However, his faith did not waiver, and in the end, God restored to him double what he had lost.

The response of religions to suffering has been varied. Some, like Buddhism, Islam and Hinduism, consider it either to be the fault of people being too attached to worldly things (Buddhism), or it is a way of submitting to the will of Allah (Islam), or it is the result of accumulated "karma" catching up with people (Hinduism).

---

[7] Archibald MacLeish, The Dialogues of Archibald MacLeish and Mark Van Doren.

Christianity alone responds to suffering by directly facing it. It uniquely alleviates suffering in all of its forms by its teachings and by meeting the much-needed physical aid caused by war and disaster, including food and water, clothing and shelter, and sanitation and medical assistance. Organizations like the American Red Cross, Salvation Army, Episcopal Relief and Development, and others, are Christian organizations. They are the first to respond to any disaster, man-made or otherwise. Many involved in the aid donate their time and expenses to the organizations. It is Christianity in shoe leather, if you will, for Christianity is much more than just those who profess the faith.

"Turn Yourself to me, and have mercy on me, for I am desolate and afflicted. The troubles of my heart have enlarged; bring me out of my distresses! Look on my affliction and my pain, and forgive all my sins." - Ps. 25:16-18.

"Hear the voice of my supplications when I cry to You, when I lift up my hands toward Your holy sanctuary." - Ps. 28:2.

"God is our refuge and strength, an ever-present help in times of trouble." - Ps. 46:1.

Christianity is founded on suffering. The blood of the martyrs is the seed of the church. Not only did Christ suffer and die, but most of the church in times past suffered and died, some by cruel torture, and many, including those up to the present day, have suffered and died in prisons for their faith.

Christians understand the ways that God works in the world, one of them being through the efforts of believers. For many Christians, helping others in times of need, have been able to help them not only materially but spiritually.

The Bible, the scepter of Christianity (Ps. 45:7), teaches that God is keenly aware of what happens to man. He knows their sufferings. He is aware of the injustices that are afflicted upon man by man. He is omniscient (for example, Ps. 139:1-4, Isa. 40:28, Heb. 4:13, and 1 John 3:30) and sovereign over all (for example, Prov. 16:33, Eph. 1:1 and Col. 1:16-17).

"The eyes of the Lord are in every place, keeping watch on the evil and the good." - Prov. 15:3.

"No creature is hidden from his sight, but all are naked and exposed to the eyes of him to whom we must give account." - Heb. 4:13.

The Bible has many examples of where faith in God brought about relief from suffering, and sometimes a miraculous cure. They include David, Hezekiah, Esther and the many deaf, blind, lame and sick who were healed by Jesus because of their faith.

The Bible is replete with verses that are very useful in times of suffering. Only one is recounted here.

"The Lord your God, who goes before you, He will fight for you, according to all He did for you in Egypt before your eyes, and in the wilderness where you saw how the Lord your God carried you, as a man carries his son, in all the way that you went until you came to this place." - Deut. 1:30-31.

It reminds me of the classic poem, "Footprints in the Sand," by Mary Stevenson.[8]

"One night I dreamed I was walking along the beach with the Lord.

---

[8] The poem is reported to have been written by Mary Stevenson in 1964.

Many scenes from my life flashed across the sky. In each scene I noticed footprints in the sand. Sometimes there were two sets of footprints, other times there were one set of footprints. This bothered me because I noticed that during the low periods of my life, when I was suffering from anguish, sorrow or defeat, I could see only one set of footprints. So I said to the Lord, "You promised me Lord, that if I followed you, you would walk with me always. But I have noticed that during the most trying periods of my life there have only been one set of footprints in the sand. Why, when I needed you most, you have not been there for me?" The Lord replied, "The times when you have seen only one set of footprints, is when I carried you."

Whenever the blood of man is spilled, it cries out to God. When Cain murdered Abel, his brother, and God asked him where his brother was, Cain said, "I do not know, am I my brother's keeper?" Then God said, "What have you done? The voice of your brother cries out to me from the ground." (Gen. 4:9-10). Other verses of the Bible also testify of the blood of man crying out to God. Deuteronomy 21:1-9 indicates that righteous blood yells for vengeance, and Revelation 6:9-11 states that the blood of innocent martyrs pleads with God to avenge it.

"Truly the hearts of the sons of men are full of evil; madness is in their hearts while they live." - Eccl. 9:3.

The Bible says in Ps. 5:5-6 that God hates all workers of iniquity and abhors the bloodthirsty and deceitful man.

"Vengeance is Mine, and recompense…for the day of their calamity is at hand, and the things to come hasten upon them." - Deut. 32:35.

"For the oppression of the poor, for the sighing of the needy, now I will arise, says the Lord." - Ps. 12:5.

"He who does wrong will be repaid for what he has done, and there is no partiality." - Col. 3:25.

"His winnowing fan is in His hand, and He will thoroughly clean out His threshing floor, and gather the wheat into His barn; but the chaff He will burn with unquenchable fire." - Luke 3:17.

It is commonly believed that everyone is intrinsically good. It is even taught in many churches. I was raised in the belief that if you wanted the best out of people then you should emphasize the best in them, but I never believed that people were intrinsically good, for there was always too much of the bad around. The notion appears to be wishful thinking more than anything else. It is the theme in many books and movies; they also depict the violent and unpredictable ways of man.

I agree that we should go through life treating people as if they were intrinsically good, but I humbly submit that the goodness of man is not what we typically observe in others. The Bible takes issue with the notion that it is man's true nature, and I believe in God more than I do public opinion. We must often look beyond wishful thinking and the mere appearance of things.

Many people do not understand how the sinful nature of man can corrupt a person's life and cause them to suffer, or cause them to treat others in heartless ways that simply defy the imagination. And most people do not want to know about such things. Nevertheless, sin in man is what has affected, and continues to significantly affect, the world and everything about it, making it suffer in one way or another, and it is what brings on wars and other vile evils that were never originally intended for man to experience.

Man's heart can be corrupted by many things, and it is amazing by how many things it may be corrupted, for sin is a powerful corrupting force. But if man recognizes his responsibility toward God and does his duty in accordance with the Holy Scriptures, his heart is protected from corruption.

The Origin of Evil

Evil began in the Garden of Eden. It was there where man first chose to go his own way without God. He ate the fruit that God had forbidden him to eat. Up until that time, which could have been many years, perhaps centuries, man lacked nothing and suffered from nothing. His punishment, however, brought on not only death, but suffering, and all the other evils that have befallen mankind. The evil became a part of man because it was a part of Adam and Eve. It passed down to every generation, and man has had to live with its terrible consequences ever since.

We know from Genesis 1:29-30 that the original food for man and beast was plants. We learn from Isaiah 65:25 that when the kingdom of God finally comes to the earth, ferocious animals will be tame, wolves and lambs will feed together, lions will eat straw like the ox, and dust will be the viper's food. Ferocious animals were not in the Garden of Eden, and they won't be during Christ's millennium reign. There is little doubt that the Garden was without plants that could hurt, but now the world is strewn with deadly plants like poison ivy and hemlock. Scripture tells us that pain and sickness arose only after Adam and Eve sinned against God (Gen. 3).

Man had once but to reach out his hand for food. After the Fall, the earth no longer yielded its fruitfulness without man's effort (Gen. 3:17-19). He must earn it as he has for thousands of years by the sweat of his brow (hard work) to provide the necessities for himself and his family.

All of nature was intrinsically good in the eyes of God when God created it (Gen. 1:9-13), but weeds and thorns sprang up after the Fall. There began a time of scarcity. Ferocious beasts roamed the earth. Pristine virgin bubbling ponds became stagnant pools infested with bacteria, viruses and mosquito larvae.

Nature groans under the weight of evil that man sent into the world, and eagerly waits for things to return to their original state (Rom. 8:20-23), which will occur when God returns to earth in His glory. It must groan even more today than previously for what man has done to her in recent years by polluting her rivers and streams and bountiful oceans and the air of the earth, and by destroying her forests and rendering large tracts of land unsuitable for growing crops.

God told Eve that from then on that He would greatly multiply her sorrow and her conception, for in pain she shall bring forth children (Gen. 3:16).

We know all too well the result of His curses. Nation is pitted against nation in disputes and wars. Everyone suffers and most everyone is bitter and resentful because of it. It is as though people instinctively realize that things should be better, that things were not meant to be way they are, and they're right. But instead of blaming ourselves, we blame God.

"Behold, I was brought forth in iniquity, and in sin my mother conceived me." - Ps. 51:5.

Is it fair to suffer the punishment given to one man, and a man that lived so long ago? One might as well ask if it is fair for a nation to suffer the consequences of decisions that are made by their governments, or question the fairness of a political party in office or the governing ruler of a nation to make decisions that affect the entire nation. The answer, of course, is that yes, these things are fair.

Adam and Eve were our first parents, our progenitors. Adam is the father of the human race. Just as we inherited traits and characteristics from our parents and grandparents, we inherited the fallen, corrupt nature of Adam and Eve, and we must face up to it.

Except for rare instances, as we will see, God has not intervened and prevented evil in any of its manifestations, but has allowed it to perpetuate and even increase; and, since Jesus Christ is the same yesterday, today and forever, it will no doubt continue to be that way until He returns. The result is that evil remains among us and continues to plague the world.

From a broader perspective, however, God *has* intervened against evil, by sacrificing His only Son on the cross to deliver His people from their bondage to the forces of evil. Jesus intervened to rescue us from our sinful natures, and His intervention came at the acceptable time (Gal. 4:4-5). His revolutionary teachings altered the course of civilization by giving hope and comfort to all souls in times of need. He altered man's understanding of evil by providing the solution for it.

The Lord is the new Adam, the new beginning of mankind, the start of a new creation, a new nation, one that is holy unto God (1 Cor. 15:45-49). Just as through one man's sin did judgment come upon all men, so through one Man's righteous act did the free gift of salvation come to all who believe in Him (Rom. 5:18-19).

God allows every person the time they need to make up their mind whether to come to know Him and accept or reject His final solution to man's problems. Meanwhile, He patiently waits with bridled vengeance and enduring forbearance, hoping, sometimes against hope, that instead of pursuing his selfish desires, man would turn to Him, for He wishes not that anyone should perish, but that all should come to repentance (2 Pet. 3:9). For this reason, He postpones His vengeance and holds out His hand to even the most evil of men until the moment of their death.

"What if God, wanting to show His wrath and to make His power known, endured with much longsuffering the vessels of wrath prepared for destruction, and that He might make known the riches of His glory on the vessels of mercy, which He had prepared beforehand for glory." - Rom. 9:22-23.

Nevertheless, it is evident that the patience of God is very near exhausted as we understand from the passage of the winnowing fan (Luke 3:17), and from Matthew 3:10, where it says the ax is already laid to the foot of the trees.

Man's purpose in life is not to struggle and die, although he does both. The Bible indicates that God made man for His purposes, and that every man, woman and child is important to Him and has dignity in His sight. It teaches that the purpose of man is to glorify God – not through divine commandment or edict, but through love.

Man is endowed with a free will; he is a free thinker. It is his free will that sets him apart, perhaps more than anything else, from all other creatures. He has been gifted with two other things as well, the breath of life and, since Jesus' time, the free gift of salvation (if only he would take hold of it). God could demand glorification from man, not only since he exists because of Him, but since He has given him every reason to glorify Him in the things He has created. However, He wants man will to come to Him and learn about Him of his own free will, and thereby fulfill the purpose for which he was created, without being coerced into it.

"The God who holds your breath in His hand and owns all your ways, you have not glorified." - Dan. 5:23.

"If He should set His heart on it, if He should gather to Himself His Spirit and His breath, all flesh would perish together, and man would return to dust." - Job 34:14-15.

"So, whether you eat or drink, or whatever you do, do all to the glory of God." - 1 Cor. 10:31.

The Devil

God also made the devil for His purposes, and He allows him to complete the work that He intended for him to do, which is to help separate believers from those who are at enmity with Him, the sheep from the goats (2 Thess. 2:7-8, Rom. 11:25, Deut. 29:29).

The word "devil" derives from the Greek word "diabolos" used in the Septuagint (the earliest extant Greek translation of the Old Testament) to translate the Hebrew word "Satan," which means adversary or enemy of God. It seems only by coincidence that the English word "devil" closely resembles the word "evil," but in my way of thinking they mean the same thing because I believe that the devil is the personification of evil.

As explained in the chapter on His Winnowing Fan, re the parable of the *Wheat and the Tares* (Matthew 13:24-30; 36-43), the kingdom of heaven is compared to a man who sowed good seed in his field. but while he slept, his enemy came and sowed tares among the wheat, and that the devil was the sower of the tares.

23

The parable explains, perhaps better than any other Scripture passage, why evil in the world has not been eliminated by God, but is tolerated by Him. Throughout history, as well as now, it is why God allows evil to exert its devastating effect on the lives of countless people.

The Bible indicates that after His Second Coming, Christ will reign on the earth for a millennium before Satan is let loose to do his works of deception again, and gather all nations to the great last battle, the battle of Armageddon (Rev. 20:1-15). The purpose of the millennial reign will be to fulfill various covenants that God made in Old Testament days to David and others. During that time, the prophecies of old, such as Isaiah 65:25, will be fulfilled.

Therefore, despite our many daily efforts, even the most commendable efforts that are made to curb the spread of evil, all of which are prized in God's sight, we can contribute but little toward relieving all of man's suffering. Evil will not go away, and we cannot we expect God to step in and prevent it from occurring, although He has done so in the past as discussed below.

Man is evil from the day he is born. All infants display, sometimes very emphatically, the urge to have their own way, and there are no exceptions, say the pediatricians and psychologists. No one is exempt from a predilection to sin, for it is a part of man's nature.

All of us are being tempted by the devil, and we can only prepare against it as best we can, but a final climax is approaching known as the Great Tribulation, and when it arrives, all that has preceded it will be but a prelude, a foretaste, of what it will be like.

When God Stepped in Against Evil

Perhaps the first instance of God stepping in against evil

occurred nine generations after Adam during the days of Noah, the son of Lamech, the son of Methuselah, the son of Enoch, the son of Jared, the son of Mahalalel, the son of Cainan, the son of Enosh, the son of Seth, the son of Adam. It was when giants lived on the earth, presumably the offspring of fallen angels (Jude 6 informs us they were angels) and their women wives (Gen. 6:4).

The evil done by them, and the concomitant evil done by the rest of the human race who were influenced by them, was so great that God relented that He had created man (Gen. 6:7).

"The Lord saw how great the wickedness of the human race had become on the earth, and that every inclination of the thoughts of the human heart was only evil all the time. The Lord regretted that he had made human beings on the earth, and his heart was deeply troubled." - Gen. 6:5-6.

Some theologians have called it an irruption of evil.[9] It brought on God's vengeance in the form of a worldwide Flood that destroyed all living creatures who dwelt above the waters of the earth, with the exception of eight souls and the animals in the ark that would later repopulate the earth. More will be said about the Great Flood later.

It also occurred when God led His chosen people by the hand of Moses, and later by Joshua, out of Egypt and into the promised land. God fought for Israel and defeated the enemies of the Lord, including most of the remnant of the giants, whose strain was not completely wiped out by the Flood but endured, apparently because the wives of the sons of Noah were among the offspring of the "daughters of man" who bore children to them (Gen. 6:4). A later chapter describes the astounding use of the Sun and Moon

---

[9] E. W. Bullinger, <u>Bullinger's Companion Bible Notes, Genesis 6</u>.

by God when He fought for Israel in this instance to defeat His enemies.

God often used the weather and other natural phenomena to change the situation, to prevent the enemies of God from gaining the victory. The stars fought against Sisera (Judg. 5:20). Lightening, thunder and great hailstones fell over Egypt when God, by the hand of Moses, liberated Israel from Pharaoh's grip (Ex. 9:23-24). Loud thunder was used to scare the Philistines (1 Sam. 7:10), and thunder and rain were used to scare Israel (1 Sam. 12:18).

The Book of Joshua gives the extraordinary account of when God stopped the Sun and the Moon for about a whole day to permit the children of Israel under Joshua to defeat their enemies. It, together with other similar miracles, are discussed in detail in a subsequent chapter.

These instances are recorded for our instruction and reproof, so that we might better understand how God reacts to evil. He can use the forces of nature to defeat His enemies or make His people change their behavior. He looks on all situations and cares for all sufferings, no matter how dire they may be, and, if possible, wants us to overcome them by our own actions.

When Peter was put in Herod's prison in Jerusalem, earnest prayer went up to God for him by the church. He was about to be sentenced the next day when he was awakened at night by an angel, his chains fell off his hands and he was led out of the prison, and when him and the angel got to the main gate of the prison, it opened of its own accord. (Acts 12:5-17).

Paul and Silas were imprisoned at Philippi after being beaten with rods by the magistrate for proclaiming the way of salvation.

Suddenly at midnight, a great earthquake shook the foundations of the prison and immediately the doors were opened and everyone's chains were loosed. (Acts 16:25-28).

Another instance of divine intervention was when Paul was stoned (you didn't get stoned without being killed). When his accusers left and his disciples came to him, he got up and walked away. (Acts 14:19-20).

In these cases, and more, we learn that suffering precedes divine deliverance. It appears to be a divine law.

Man is wondrously made and capable of performing the most stupendous feats, not only in sports but in the arts, sciences and industry. His remarkable intelligence and physical prowess have overcome practically every obstacle imposed by nature or man. However, his abilities can be used for malevolent purposes. Man seems to have a yen for war, and is fascinated by it. The reason is that despite all the good that is in man, there is a dark and fearsome side, a side that is so evil that many of us shun the very thought of its bottomless depths, making us capable of inflicting the vilest of cruelties on our fellowman.

Regarding the evil that men do, Solomon said that it is better to be unborn than those that died under oppression and the oppressed. "Better than both is he who has not yet been and has not seen the evil deeds that are done under the Sun." - Eccl. 4:3.

Jesus' resurrection and the testimony of those who saw Him afterwards made such an impact on the world that it changed the way time is specified, dividing it into two parts, "AD" and "BC." AD, which stands for *Anno Domini*, or *in the year of our Lord*, denotes the time after Jesus' birth, and "BC," which stands for "Before Christ," denotes the time before His birth.

The raising of Jesus from the dead was the birth of Christianity. It also ushered in the Holy Spirit's presence and power in the world, which apparently, according to the Divine Word, was, generally speaking, absent from the world, although some were given it before, such as those who saved and judged Israel in the Book of Judges, and the prophets of old.

"And when He [the Holy Spirit] has come, He will convict the world of sin, and of righteousness, and of judgment: of sin, because they do not believe in Me; of righteousness, because I go to My Father and you see Me no more; of judgment, because the ruler of this world is judged." - John 16:8-12.

Before the resurrection of Christ, the conscience was the only thing that would convict a person of sin, but afterwards, as now, it is not only conscience that can convict one of sin, but also the work that the Holy Spirit does in the world. More will be said about the Spirit of God later.

The Evils of Sickness, Disease and Heartbreak

Plagues (now called pandemics), often scourge the world, but sickness, disease and heartbreak are the common lot of man, for everyone suffers them sooner or later.

It is not unusual for people to think that health problems, especially those of long duration, are brought on by God, either for sins committed (John 9:1-2), for testing of faith (James 1:2-3; 1 Pet. 1:7) or for chastening (Heb. 12:7-12). As a result, some of us are more inclined to acquiesce to health issues than take the proper steps that would remedy or cure them, especially if they require much personal effort.

God indeed tests our faith and chastens those whom He loves (Hebrews 12:5-11). But chastening can take on many forms, and perhaps each is chosen to have a unique effect on the individual's growth and well-being, in material as well as spiritual ways. With the exception of being cast down and stricken by God for purposes of bringing us to our knees and repentance, it is hard for me to believe that a holy God desires that man, His favorite creation (Gen. 1:26-37), should suffer illness, disease and premature death, for it is written that His rod and His staff comfort us (Ps. 23), and each of us already suffers, and will continue to suffer in many ways, because of our inadequacies and sins.

I believe that we must never let unanswered prayer come between us and the goodness of God. It has been my experience and observation that we are more than capable of causing our own sicknesses. We unwittingly bring sickness and disease upon ourselves through dietary practices that are contrary to the laws of nature. For example, it is a well-known fact that saturated fats in the diet raise LDL (bad) cholesterol levels and cause the formation of fatty deposits in the arteries, which causes atherosclerosis and high blood pressure, and heart disease.

That is not to say that disease and death do not come to heathy people, because they do, but many of the troubles we have can be avoided through education, sanitation and proper dietary practices.

Perhaps one should pray not so much for the removal of a health issue as for the wisdom to know how to change it. Very often, all that is needed to resolve a health issue is to change something about the way we are living. A change in diet is often required to correct a health issue. But whatever the disease or sickness, God would want us to utilize our own abilities at problem solution.

Then there are the many heartbreaks and calamities of life that everyone experiences sooner or later, such as the loss of a loved one, a financial disaster, divorce, traumatic injury and physical or mental handicap. Is it realistic to ask ourselves whether sufferings are fair? It's like saying, "Is it fair for a person to get a disease of which they are inclined or dispositioned to get?" Or, "Is it fair for people to die?" These are just the way things are.

The natural man, which is the average man, is at enmity with God, at continual war with Him, unless he is moved by the Spirit of God to accept the truth about Jesus Christ (John 6:44). The natural man is spiritually blind; the Word and the things of the Spirit of God are foolishness to him; neither can he know them, because they are spiritually discerned (1 Cor. 2:14). All he can see is the material world, the things of the world, the things that make for his comfort and pleasure – things that can be seen and felt. We are living spiritual lives in a darkened world.

"For he stretches out his hand against God, and acts defiantly against the Almighty, running stubbornly against Him with his strong, embossed shield." - Job 15:25-26.

Of these things we are certain. They have, from the beginning, established two great and enduring moral principles – right and wrong, and it is the struggle between them that has continued down through the ages to this day, and no doubt will continue as long as man is on the earth.

As nations of the world, such as former Soviet Russia (Russia) and Communist China (China)[10] continue to collaborate against the West, our efforts to advance democracy and human rights continue to be thwarted. You cannot make treaties with people

---

[10] To this day, China remains communist.

whose political dogmas are diametrically opposed to yours, for they will not be honored, because it is the nature of man to mistrust others, and it is the nature of Communist nations to serve no other purposes but their own.

When David came to the camp of Israel when it faced the Philistines in battle array and heard Goliath's challenge that Israel send a man to fight him, the giant said that if a man from Israel defeated him, then all the Philistines would become their servants, but if he defeated Israel's man, then the Israelites must serve them. However, after David slew the giant, the Philistines fled and did not honor the contract (1 Sam. 17: 8-9).

"Take heed to yourself, lest you make a covenant with the inhabitants of the land where you are going, lest it be a snare in your midst." - Ex. 34:12.

A gardener knows that if flowers are always kept in the green house and raised in warm temperatures, they cannot live outdoors. Therefore, he does not give them too much heat, and by degrees exposes them to the cold so that eventually they can survive in the open air. God does not keep us unexposed to trials, but as explained in Hebrews 12:5-11 and mentioned previously, He chastens those whom He loves.

We must run with footmen to be able to contend with horses. We must be thrown into the water or we'll never learn to swim. We must suffer before we learn how to overcome our difficulties. For we are tempered by trials and sufferings. Although it may feel like we're being forged in the fire, it is God's way of strengthening us through the filling up of the sufferings of Christ and the testing of our faith (Col. 1:24, James 1:3. 1 Pet. 1:7). And let us not forget that we have not yet resisted to bloodshed, striving against sin as did our Lord (Heb. 12:3-4).

Chapter 3 The Value of Suffering

"Why are you cast down, O my soul? And why are you disquieted within me? Hope in God; for I shall yet praise Him, the help of my countenance and my God." - Ps. 43:5.

The purpose of this chapter is to describe perhaps the only bright side to suffering. While I believe that suffering is part and parcel of this life, an inescapable part of the human condition, I also believe that it has more value than what most people claim, such as the benefit that may be derived from sharing our grief with family members or others. I also believe it has more value than the spiritual benefits we glean from Scripture, namely those deriving from enduring God's chastening and sharing in Jesus's sufferings (2 Cor. 1:5, Phil. 3:10, Col. 1:24, 1 Pet. 4:13).

Pain and suffering are hard taskmasters, but they can be the only teachers we ever listen to long enough to change something critical about ourselves so that our conditions improve. I believe that the benevolent God knew at the Fall that all suffering had this kind of value for man.

People don't usually question themselves or the world, or consider change to be necessary and start to work on themselves until they are struck by some form of suffering. They seldom if ever follow the simple aphorism, "nothing ventured, nothing gained," but nurse their unfortunate state as best they can and remain in despair. Many keep within their time-worn patterns of living, trapped because of habit, and are unable to see the beacon of warning that something must change if they ever hope to get better.

Solomon, the wisest man ever to have lived, told us what wisdom is. For one, it is the fear of God (Prov. 9:10, Eccl. 12:13). It is also found in enjoying whatever good comes to us, and in considering why, when evil or adversity or suffering comes, it comes, and what may be gained from it (Eccl. 7:14). Is it not to instruct us to make preparations so that it does not recur? As harsh weather forces us to make preparations to endure it, so with adversity, for it strengthens us. It improves us in some way. It makes us better than we were before – does it not?

"Wisdom strengthens the wise more than ten rulers of the city." - Eccl. 7:19.

The Bible emphasizes the importance of taking appropriate action within a reasonable time, and the error of doing nothing. It is expressed throughout the Word, for example in Ex. 18:17-21, Eccl. 9:10, Col.3:23-24, James 2:14-18, 1 John 3:18, and in the many of the parables of Jesus, which are the subject of another chapter.

There are always many remedial solutions open to us, but many people become so stuck in their ways that they unwittingly bring further suffering upon themselves, and cause others to suffer, because of inaction, their unwillingness to change something about themselves that may or would improve their condition.

Although not in the Bible, an appropriate saying is, "God helps those who help themselves." After experiencing much personal suffering, I would not hesitate to advise that people spend more time trying to help themselves. We should pray unceasingly (1 Thess. 5:16-18), but prayer should not take the place of action.

Suffering can result in self-education, learning about things never learned before. When knowledge replaces ignorance, the formerly unknown becomes known; then we have the power to solve problems, which enables us to get on with life.

The evils that befall us often give us a purpose, an objective, we didn't have before. Our goals change us. Reaching them establishes us. The best thing we can do when we suffer is to ask ourselves, how can I get over it or make it go away, for by discovering why we are suffering we can often do something about it.

The extent of a person's sufferings may be great, as is typically the case for those who have lost a child, or have experienced the horrors of war, or suffer from a crippling disease like rheumatoid arthritis or gout, or are going through chemotherapy for some type of cancer. We never really know how much something is worth to us until we lose it. However, we must believe that there is a reason, or root cause, for our suffering, for there is a reason for everything in God's world, and if there is a reason then there must be a purpose for it. In many cases, the purpose for suffering is to alert us to a danger that is not likely to go away unless we do something about it, something that addresses the reason for its existence.

Everyone seeks answers during times of suffering, and the more intense the suffering the more we are on our knees, but many people need to actively dig further for the answers. Very few people are ever miraculously healed, and to remedy the condition usually means keep searching for the answers. God hears our prayers and promises to answer them (Luke 11:9-10, Luke 12:48, James 1:5-8).

Jesus Christ has never changed. Prayer is as answerable today as it ever was, and the days of miracles have not passed, but are forever possible through the exercise of faith in Him. He knows the causes of and the cures for everything, and much of it is revealed in some way in His Word. Seek and you shall find (Matt. 7:7, Luke 11:9). When we pray, we need to be alert to, and receptive of, the ways in which He answers it. Sometimes an idea will pop into the mind and you'll realize it is something that must be acted on. I have seen it happen within a few minutes of earnest prayer, but an answer will come, and when it does, you will wonder why you never thought of it before.

In times of suffering, it is best to lay everything out before Him. Earnestly ask Him for the wisdom and direction on how to proceed, and you will get an answer. But be careful how the request is phrased. It should be a simple but exact statement of what you want God to do for you. For example, if you pray for relief from some troublesome issue, then it may be relieved for a while but still continue to manifest itself. However, if you pray for the wisdom and direction that will gain victory over it, God may give you the solution directly, or else guide you to it.

When Jacob prayed to God to deliver him from the hand of his brother Esau after he learned that he was coming with four-hundred armed men to meet him (Gen. 32:11), God answered his prayer by making him less of a threat to Esau. He crippled him, making him lean on his staff, and he limped on his hip from then on (Gen. 32:31).

We must trust the Word of God.

"If any of you lacks wisdom, let him ask of God, who gives to all liberally and without reproach, and it will be given to him. But let him ask in faith, with no doubting, for he who doubts is like a wave of the sea driven and tossed by the wind. For let not that man suppose that he will receive anything from the Lord; he is a double-minded man, unstable in all his ways." - James 1:5-8.

In addition to prayer, we can all look to Scriptures for comfort.

"In the multitude of my anxieties within me, Your comforts delight my soul." - Ps. 94:19.

The Scripture passage that has helped me more than most to unravel the reason for my sufferings is Prov. 3:5-6:

"Trust in the Lord with all your heart, and lean not on your own understanding. In all your ways acknowledge Him, and He shall direct your paths." - Prov. 3:5-6.

Personal suffering enables us to understand the strengths and weaknesses of ourselves as we grapple with solutions. It is then that we can see some good in suffering. However, it must be emphasized that if a do-nothing attitude is adopted about suffering, we may never discover many of our strengths and weaknesses, for it is through trial and error, sometimes fiery trial and error, that situations are improved.

Without suffering, we would be without the testing of faith that so tempers or strengthens us. We would be without the virtues of character, perseverance and hope, which are gained in times of suffering, and we would likely be unappreciative of the many things that we take for granted (Rom. 5:3), the simple things of life, like air and water, the time it takes for a day to pass, the work others do, and the value of rest and of life itself.

Without suffering, there would be little need for change, and without change there would be little improvement in our conditions. Despair, helplessness and pain, like their opposites, joy, independence and pleasure, can serve as the impetus or driving force that gets us on our feet to solve our problems.

"I can bear witness that trials are a great blessing. I would not have learned much except for trouble and painful difficulty." - Charles H. Spurgeon, *Beside Still Waters.*

In times of trouble and fear, when nothing seems to help, we are not to give in or give up on the problem, but stay in the game, continuing to do our duty as best as we can.

Do not forget that prayer can give the direction one needs to resolve the difficulty. But you say, I have prayed to God to take this or that burden/disappointment/sorrow/heartbreak away, but with no result. Again, be careful of how your prayers are worded. If you want and expect God to do what you say, then lift them up to Him as precisely as you can.

Sometimes the answer arrives in the early morning hours and causes us to wake up and jot it down (Ps. 16:7). At other times it comes by way of a dream.

"In a dream, in a vision of the night, when deep sleep falls upon men, while slumbering on their beds, then He opens the ears of men, and seals their instruction." - Job 33:15-16.

By acting on these principles, many of the problems of life may be solved.

"In the dangers we run in this life, how wonderfully we are delivered when we know nothing of it; how, when we are in a quandary, as we call it, a doubt or hesitation whether to go this way or that way, a secret hint shall direct us this way, when we intended to go that way; nay, when sense, our own inclination, and perhaps business has called us to go the other way, yet a strange impression upon the mind, from we know not what springs, and by we know not what power, shall overrule us to go this way, and it shall afterward appear that had we gone that way, which we should have gone, and even to our imagination ought to have gone, we should have been ruined and lost." - Daniel Defoe, *Robinson Crusoe*.

God wants us to talk to Him all the time. When convinced of this truth, we pray more often, which drastically changes our lives.

"O Master, let me walk with Thee
in lonely paths of service free,
Tell me Thy secret, help me to bear,
The strain of toil, the fret of care."[11]

Earnest prayer has turned sadness into joy for many people many times by providing the direction needed to solve a particular problem. Prayer can raise one up above their pain/distress/ despair/heartbreak to light and gladness. But only by way of action, not inaction, not do-nothingness, is it possible for many things to improve. For God helps those who help themselves.

J. Vernon McGee put it this way:

"When a man prays for a corn crop, He expects him to say Amen with a hoe."

God may not prevent suffering, but many are the merciful dispositions of heaven. I thank God for the difficulties that have taught me the hard way how to improve my life.

It may take much soul searching and reflection to come to terms with a troublesome issue, especially one that so torments that it

---

[11] The Christian Hymn, O Master, let me walk with Thee, was written by Washington Gladden in 1879.

seems impossible to reconcile or resolve. It may require a new approach, one you never thought of before – and it usually does. It may require study and expenditure of time, money and effort, but as long as we believe that there is a purpose or a reason for it then we have a good chance to discover what that reason is and use it for our betterment.

The apostle Paul kept recounting what he had gone through – calamities that burdened him beyond measure, above strength, and even to the point of despairing life, itself, including chains, imprisonments, stonings, beatings, shipwrecks where he had spent a night and a day in the deep, scarcity of food, scarcity of water, scarcity of sleep, and the scarcity of clothing and shelter – but he considered them all as rubbish compared to gaining Christ (Phil. 3:8, 2 Cor. 11:25, 2 Cor. 1:8, Rom. 8:18).

All suffering is relative.[12] But one thing is universal. Without it we would never approach the throne room of God, for our pride would never allow that to happen. God does not require an "at-one-ment" (atonement) for our sins through any efforts of our own, including penance or some other self-achieved means, which is not possible in any event. It is only possible through the grace of God by way of His Son, who is our atonement. All we have to do to be reconciled to Him is believe in His Son.

We mustn't forget the enormous suffering that was forced upon our Lord, not only the physical suffering He endured through the pain of scourging and the Cross, but that which He bore that no one else has or ever will bear – the sins of the whole world (John 1:29). Can anyone imagine what it must be like to take on the awful sins of everyone past, present and future?

---

[12] Victor Frankel stated that the "size" of human suffering is relative.

Chapter 4 Christ Brings Division

"I came to send fire on the earth, and how I wish it were already kindled! But I have a baptism to be baptized with, and how distressed I am till it is accomplished! Do you suppose that I came to give peace on earth? I tell you, not at all, but rather division. For from now on five in one house will be divided: three against two, and two against three. Father will be divided against son and son against father, mother against daughter and daughter against mother, mother-in-law against her daughter-in-law and daughter-in-law against her mother-in-law." - Luke 12:49-53.

The rather long passage is an astonishingly personal statement from the lips of Jesus about why He came into the world. The message is stated even stronger in Matthew:

"Do not think that I have come to bring peace to the earth; I have not come to bring peace, but a sword." - Matt. 10:34.

It is not a warning, but a simple statement of fact. It gives us profound truth. It no doubt startled everyone who heard it when He preached it, and no one questioned Him about it.

From the start of the Gospels we are confronted with the fact that Jesus brings division, for it is what jumps out at us at the beginning of the Gospel of Matthew. Immediately following the story of Jesus's birth we read about the plan to destroy the child and the slaughter of the innocents in Bethlehem by order of Herod. It is the beginning of the division.

In the passage of Luke we see that Jesus wishes that His final mission was already completed – that of sending fire to the earth, which will take place in the Day of the Lord when He returns to the earth the second time. It is only then that we may proceed to the Day of Judgment, when all souls will be judged, and then to fulfilling the goal that God has had from the foundation of the world – the fulfillment of the establishment of the kingdom of heaven. But first, He must go to the cross, the baptism that He must be baptized with.

Like the message of the winnowing fan, Christ's message of division is difficult for many people to understand. It seems so atypical of Jesus' doctrine of love and peace which is so much heard about today. It shows the stern side of God, the side that most people would rather not see.

The Bible is our standard for truth, and everything it says about Jesus is true. He is the firstborn over all creation (Col. 1:15). He is unchangeable in His love and care for us (John 3:1, 3:16 and 4:16). In Him is found all the grace, love, compassion, wisdom, power and understanding of the Godhead (Col. 1:15). But He is also a great King.

Jesus does bring peace (Isa. 32:17, Gal. 5:22-23, John 16:33, Rom. 5:1), but it is peace between God and man. It is inner peace, spiritual peace (Phil. 4:7), not worldly peace; and it is not for everyone for His peace is for those with whom He is pleased. Both the NRSV and HCSB versions of Luke 2:14 state similarly, "Glory to God in the highest heaven, and peace on earth to people He favors," which I believe is the correct rendering. The same idea was expressed by the angel sent from God to Joseph before Jesus's birth, announcing that He would "save His people from their sins."

He came to establish a division among men, not one based on pride and arrogance, as most worldly divisions are based, but on belief in Him. It was a new and radical doctrine portending enormous social change by way of friction and strife between family members and nations.

The dichotomy places all of humanity into two groups or classes – those who are for Him and those who are against Him. "He who is not with Me is against Me, and he who does not gather with Me scatters abroad." (Matt. 12:30). We are either on the Lord's side or Satan's side. No middle or neutral ground is possible.

There are many absolutes in life, such as right and wrong, good and evil, light and darkness, holy and profane, just as there are absolutes in afterlife. We see another here, wheat and tares.

The Bible assures us that no peace can exist on earth as long as sin is in the world. As stated throughout the Bible, God hates sin and all of its manifestations,[13] for behind it is enmity against Him (Rom. 8:7 and James 4:4). Like the absolutes of heaven and hell, Jesus proclaimed that everyone is either God's friend or His enemy. This "either-or" doctrine, having no middle or neutral ground, is common in the Scriptures. Just two examples are:

"See, I have set before you today life and good, death and evil, in that I command you today to love the Lord your God, to walk in His ways, and to keep His commandments, His statutes, and His judgments, that you may live and multiply; and the Lord your God will bless you in the land which you go to possess. But if your heart turns away so that you do not hear, and are drawn away, and worship other gods and serve them, I announce to you today that you shall surely perish." - Deut. 30:15-18.

"Whoever confesses Me before men, him I will also confess

---

[13] For example, in Ps. 5:5-6, Ps. 11:5, Ps. 34:16, Ps. 101:3, Prov. 6:16-19, and Zech. 8:17.

before My Father who is in heaven. But whoever denies Me before men, him I will also deny before My Father who is in heaven." - Matt. 10:32-33.

We live an age of tolerance, one that fosters very few absolutes. A common belief throughout the world is that everything is relative, beliefs as well as conduct, that what is considered good and evil, or right and wrong depend on the situation and the individual. It's a view that is based on public opinion, which is contrary to Holy Writ. The Bible tells us that man's heart is desperately wicked (Jer. 17:9), and his inclination is only to sin (Gen. 6:5, Gen. 8:21, Mark 7:21, 2 Pet. 2:14).

"What right have you to declare My statutes, or take My covenant in your mouth, seeing you hate instruction and cast My words behind you?" - Ps. 50:16-17.

"You love evil more than good, and lying more than speaking the truth." - Ps. 52:2.

The mirror that Christianity holds up to people is not what people want to see. They do not want to be confronted with or reminded of their sins, for most people are perfectly content to remain in them. Nor do they want to hear about divine judgement, but only want to be assured that they are the masters of their fate.

People typically plan everything as though this life was the sum total of their existence. It leads to a lack of attention and preparation for needs of the soul.

The by-word of today is "live and let live." The aphorism, "to err is human," suggests that it is only natural and therefore acceptable for people to err. If everyone's doing it, the tendency of most people is to see nothing wrong with it. But that is not what the

Bible teaches. We have changed the moral code of the Bible to fit our behavior, instead of changing our behavior to fit the moral code. It was the sin of man in the Book of Genesis, the sin of those in Israel and Judea as recorded in the Book of Judges, and it is our sin today. It's the "broad road" view that follows the crowd, going where it goes and doing what it does (Matt. 7: 13-14).

But Jesus wants us to be stand out from the crowd, to be different. He wants His people to expose wrongs, not condone them.

We need to see the world as it is, and God in His Word wants us to know the world as it is and how Satan is the god of it (2 Cor. 4:4). Keeping this in mind makes us more realistic, less tolerant and more observant witnesses of what happens in the world.

Those who preach the Word will have a tough time. The Bible tells us that Satan, the deceiver of the whole world, and his accomplices, are enraged against those who keep the commandments of God and have the testimony of Jesus Christ (Rev. 12:17). Ministers of Jesus will be hated by men who will scorn and separate them from their company. But great is their reward in heaven.

"Blessed are you when people hate you, when they exclude you and insult you and reject your name as evil, because of the Son of Man. Rejoice in that day and leap for joy, because great is your reward in heaven. For that is how their ancestors treated the prophets." - Luke 6:22-23.

"Blessed are those who are persecuted for righteousness' sake, For theirs is the kingdom of heaven." - Matthew 5:10.

"And behold, I am coming quickly, and My reward is with Me, to give to every one according to his work." - Rev. 22:12.

The division brought about by Jesus is one of the main purposes for His coming to earth. It was a purpose God intended from the foundation of the world. It was His purpose for the children of Abraham and Israel (Lev. 20:26), and it continues to be His purpose today. It is fulfilled when the gospel is spread through the world. It is confessed by us every time we say the Lord's prayer ("...Your will be done on earth as it is in heaven."). God wants His chosen ones, His people (Matt. 1:21), those with whom He is pleased (Luke 2:14), those that do His will, to be set apart as a holy people, a nation unto Him (2 Tim. 1:9).

"But you are a chosen generation, a royal priesthood, a holy nation, His own special people, that you may proclaim the praises of Him who called you out of darkness into His marvelous light." - 1 Pet. 2:9, and similarly 2 Tim. 1:9.

How Division Reflects the Afterlife

It is apparent from Scripture that one of the intents and designs of God is that there be a separation of kind on earth that reflects the separation of kind that exists in the afterlife. It is reflected, for example, in Heb. 8:5:

"They [the priests] serve at a sanctuary that is a copy and shadow of what is in heaven. This is why Moses was warned when he was about to build the tabernacle: "See to it that you make everything according to the pattern shown you on the mountain." - Heb. 8:5.

We are to understand that the tabernacle of Moses was patterned after what exists already in heaven, the details of which are hidden from us but it is obvious that they include each of the items that were positioned behind the veil, in the holy of holies part of the tabernacle, and that they suggest and represent, in some figurative way perhaps, the way things are in heaven.

Accordingly, and in concert with the Holy Scriptures, the division of wheat and tares on earth, instituted by Jesus, reflects the way things are in the afterlife, namely, that there are two kinds of afterlife, heaven and hell.

We also lean from Scripture that the occupants of heaven and hell are chiefly determined by man. Exceptions are Satan and the other fallen angels who were destined for hell when they were forced out of heaven (Rev. 12:3-4). In other words, man determines his own eternal destiny, for God's gift of free choice allows him to choose the way he will go (Sir. 15:14).

It is a serious mistake to allow oneself (not to mention a congregation), to get into a position that could jeopardize its eternal future, for drastically different are the two alternatives and fleeting is this life in comparison.

The way man treats God and His Son, and how he treats others, determines his eternal destination. This is important to understand, for many people believe that it is God who sends souls to heaven or hell, and many believe He does it arbitrarily. God owns the soul (Ezek. 18:4) and can destroy it in hell (Matt. 10:28, Matt. 25:46), but He does not directly determine where each soul goes after mortal death. While it is His design to divide the human race into two classes, His design also is that man determines his own ultimate destiny. It is how God wants it.

His judgement is based on what each person does and does not do, says and does not say, and believes and does not believe. It is why the souls of the unborn (preborn) and infants are ushered into heaven, for they have not been given the cognizance to discern between their right hand and their left (Jonah 4:11). They never reach the mental capacity to respond to the gospel of Jesus Christ. "Their angels always see the face of My Father who is in heaven." - Matt. 18:10.

St. Augustine said, "A man who uses free choice badly loses both himself and free choice."

Those who belong to the truth hear His voice (John 18:37), are drawn to Him by faith and guided by the Holy Spirit (John 6:44, John 14:26), and they follow Him, but those who do not hear His voice are slaves of the evil one, for their hearts have grown dull, their ears are hard of hearing, and their eyes are closed (Matt. 13:13-15). It is from these two types of people, seen in the eyes of God as sheep and goats, that heaven and hell will be populated.

As indicated in the chapter on Suffering, when Christ returns to the earth for His millennial reign, Satan will be let loose to do his works of deception once again, and gather all nations to the great last battle, Armageddon (Rev. 20:1-15). It will be a second winnowing of the wheat from the chaff, indicating, once again, the importance of division in meeting the purposes of God.

God's spiritual kingdom of benevolence, the kingdom of heaven, is a kingdom of peace (Rom. 14:7). It is the kind of peace that, deep-down, everyone is trying to secure. It is what everyone yearns for. But the peace of God that all believers in Christ have does not exclude them from being persecuted or hated by the world. In fact, it guarantees it.

Many Christians pray thinking of the blessings that will come their way, but Jesus never promised only blessings. The road He travelled was unpaved and deeply rutted with suffering and pain, disappointment and sorrow. Can we, as followers of Christ, expect things to be any different? Paul said not in his epistles, and Jesus forewarned His disciples in various passages, such as Matt. 10:21-22, of what lay ahead of them – imprisonment, torture and death, and all for their not being part of this world, but being a part of a heavenly world, a spiritual kingdom of holiness.

Jesus is the Prince of Peace (Isa. 9:6). But His first coming was not for the purpose of bringing peace to the earth, but division. He said:

"If I had not come and spoken to them, they would have no sin, but now they have no excuse for their sin. He who hates Me hates My Father also. If I had not done among them the works which no one else did, they would have no sin; but now they have seen and also hated both Me and My Father." - John 15:22-23.

Jesus' discourses with the Pharisees and other Jews always angered them in some way. Some of His words angered them so much that they were determined to kill Him. An example is given in the Book of John when Jesus proclaimed that He was the good shepherd and that this command He received from His Father:

"Some who heard this said with great anger: 'He is demon-possessed and raving mad. Why listen to him?'" - John 10:20.

The raising of Lazarus from the dead intensified the hostility of the rulers against Jesus. Their anger also extended to Lazarus, for they plotted his death and no doubt carried it out immediately after Jesus' crucifixion.

"If the world hates you, you know that it hated Me before it hated you." - John 15:18.

Jesus and His Word causes division.

As revealed in the lives of the apostles, everything that Jesus told them came true. They were cast out, stoned, imprisoned, tortured and killed – all because of their teaching and spreading the gospel to the Jews and Gentiles. The world itself was being "turned upside down" because of their teachings (Acts 17:6).

What followed was a long succession of martyrs of Jesus, from Polycarp and Justin Martyr to Cyprian to Ignatius of Antioch, to Pelagia of Tarsus, to Sadok and the Dominican martyrs from the Sandomierz to Sir Thomas More, William Tyndale, John Hooper and Francis Taylor to the Martyrs of Japan to the Canadian Martyrs to the Korean Martyrs, to Edith Stein to Dietrich Bon-hoeffer, to the Martyrs of Albania, to Jim Elliot, Martin Luther King, Jr. and Ita Ford, and many, many more. The blood of the martyrs is the seed of the Church.

By the saints of the past, present and future, the word of the Lord runs swiftly and is glorified, fulfilling the Great Commission (Matt. 28:19-20, Mark 16:15), but it causes division.

Jesus preached to relatively few people, and most of the time to a mere handful of men. His charge of spreading the Word was made to less than five hundred brethren,[14] but it was through them that the gospel spread to the entire world. He had come into the world that the world through Him might be saved (John 3:17), and

---

[14] According to Acts 1:3, Jesus was seen by the apostles for 40 days after rising from the grave, and Paul tells us in 1 Cor. 15:6 that more than five hundred brethren saw Him during that time.

these first missionaries were tasked with doing their part to ensure that it would be carried out.

Since that time, the world has been torn apart by man's reactions to the Word of God. Unrepentant man is at war with God – those who reject the only way of salvation through Jesus (John 14:6, Rom. 5:1).

A believer is called to love God and His Son above all things, including family and friends. This creates friction and conflict, for when the message of the gospel is heard quarrels and divisions abound.

"Brother will deliver up brother to death, and a father his child; and children will rise up against parents and cause them to be put to death. And you will be hated by all for My name's sake. But he who endures to the end will be saved. - Matt. 10:21-22.

What happens in families happens in neighborhoods, and what happens in neighborhoods happens in towns and cities, and likewise in counties, states and nations.

"If you were of the world, the world love its own. Yet because you are not of the world, but I chose you out of the world, therefore the world hates you…If they persecuted Me, they will also persecute you…But all these things they will do to you for My name's sake, because they do not know Him who sent Me." - John 15:19-21.

Resentment, anger and wrath have always been the first reactions to Christianity. Another is ridicule. Christian beliefs, like virgin birth, a defeated man dying on a cross (and a king at that!), rebirth and the miracles of Christ, simply do not register well with most people. Being foreign to commonsense and logic, they upset their sentiments. Miracles to most people are simply coincidences, chance occurrences, and are not of divine origin.

"The natural man does not receive the things of the Spirit of God, for they are foolishness to him; nor can he know them, because they are spiritually discerned." - 1 Cor. 2:14.

Christianity is a separatist religion. It sets itself apart from all other belief systems. The idea of believers being separate from others pervades all of Scripture (e.g., Gen. 49:26, Lev. 15:31, Lev. 20:26, Ezra 10:11, and 2 Cor. 6:17). It is what God fully intended to be accomplished through His Son.

A Christian is a separated man. He is separated forever unto God (1 Peter 2:9). He stands alone in the world and is set apart from others to serve the purposes of God. The sanest person in the world is a Christian, for he or she understands God's purposes for the world. They alone know the reason for their existence, the truth about life, where they came from and where they are going, because the God gives them the knowledge when they acknowledge the truth about Jesus. It separates them from others like nothing else can, and the difference can, and does, incur resentment and wrath.

Jesus taught that one's spiritual status, one's relationship to God is what is of supreme importance in life. It is what's needed above all other things, and when it is gained it shall not be taken away (Luke 10:42).

Christianity teaches peace, not war. But the religion is easily construed to be unfriendly because of what many perceive is a "holier than thou" attitude on the part of Christians. It can turn off others because it appears to elevate believers to a status superior to them, which, of course, is not true. One must be careful not to give that impression or cross that thin line, for no one has an exclusive right to God or a monopoly on Him.

The division that Jesus brought to earth fostered a history of wars and aggressions between believers in Christ and those in opposition ever since Jesus went to the cross, for two reasons: first because whatever man does is right in his own eyes, even when he defends religion, and second, because, as Jesus said in His message of division, the world is in opposition to Him and those who believe in Him. Just one example is the Crusades, a series of religious wars that were initiated and supported by the Church for many years during the medieval era.

No, despite the good intentions of many in the church, Jesus does not bring peace on earth, but division between the righteous and unrighteous, between the sheep and goats, between those who will dwell with Him in heaven and those who will suffer eternal damnation with the devil and his angels in hell.

"Those who honor me I will honor, and those who despise me shall be treated with contempt." - 1 Sam. 2:30.

"You are justified in Your sentence and blameless when You pass judgement." - Ps. 51:4.

"When the wicked spring up like grass, and when all the workers of iniquity flourish, it is that they may be destroyed forever." - Ps. 92:7.

"What shall we say then? Is there unrighteousness with God? Certainly not! For He says to Moses, "I will have mercy on whomever I will have mercy, and I will have compassion on whomever I will have compassion." - Rom. 9:14-15.

Chapter 5 The Wrath of God

The wrath of God is revealed not only in the passages of Scripture like the winnowing fan and division, but in many places throughout its pages. God' supreme sovereignty over man and all that He created is a principal theme of the Bible. As echoed throughout the Bible, the Lord will take vengeance on his enemies and those who are disobedient to His Word.

Before discussing this issue, however, we need to settle a question that many people have difficulty with, and that is, if God loves everyone (and He does), then why doesn't everyone go to heaven when they die? Or, put another way, parents typically overlook the bad things that kids do and love them anyway, so why doesn't God love us despite our sins?

The same people tend to forget that He is a righteous God who hates disobedience and evil, which is sin against God.

"Has the Lord as great delight in burnt offerings and sacrifices as in obeying the voice of the Lord? Behold, to obey is better than sacrifice, and to heed than the fat of rams." - 1 Sam. 15:22.

"But your iniquities have made a separation between you and your God, and your sins have hidden His face from you so that He does not hear." - Isa. 59:2.

They also tend to forget that He loved us so much that He sent His one and only Son into the world to die on the cross for us. As Paul said:

"God shows his love for us in that while we were still sinners, Christ died for us." - Rom. 5:8.

While God is love (1 John 4:8), He is also holy and just. In the Garden of Eden, when God commanded Adam and Eve not to eat of the Tree of Life after giving them a paradise world to live in, and they broke the command through the deceitfulness of the serpent, He had no choice but to punish them, and punish them He did.

When God gave Israel the commandments, ordinances and precepts of the Law, He repeatedly told them that if they failed to follow them and continued to worship other gods like all the other nations, and refused to be a people different from all others in a country that He had given to them, then He would take away their many blessings, send curses upon them and drive them from the promised land. He had no choice but to do so when they turned their backs on Him, reverted to heathenism and sacrificed their children to foreign gods.

Because the words of the Bible proceed out of the mouth of God (Matt. 4:4), every form of evil cannot, and will not, go unpunished. God cannot lie (Num. 23:19, Titus 1:2, Heb. 6:8), and He will do everything He says He will do. Many people stumble over this fact because they do not wish to believe that God is a God of wrath.

As described in the Bible and discussed in the chapter on Suffering, God has shown His great vengeance on the world many times in the past, and all of them are recorded for our instruction and reproof, so that we might better understand who He is and how He reacts to sin.

The Destruction of Jerusalem

The wrath of God is perhaps best illustrated by the Great Flood, which will be discussed in another chapter. But it is also vividly illustrated by the destruction of Jerusalem that occurred twice in its tumultuous history, when God employed the armies of the

Babylonians (the first time) and the Romans (the second time) to array themselves against it and destroy it. It clearly shows the patience and forbearance, but the eventual vengeance, of the Lord on disobedience and evil. It shows also how He typically carries out His stern warnings – through the actions of nations.

"When God comes forth in wrath, the hills tremble, fear seizes even great men. When God designs the ruin of a provoking people, He can find instruments to be employed in it." - Matthew Henry.[15]

It's first destruction is principally told in the Old Testament Books of Isaiah and Jerimiah. It was a fulfillment of prophesy that had been given to the people through God's prophets years before its destruction in 589–587 B.C. The defenders were slaughtered, the women ravished, the infants were dashed on the rocks, homes were burned and the walls were broken down. Except for those who died on the way from disease or starvation, the rest were carried off to Babylon and to various parts thereof.

When the Romans under Titus Caesar leveled Jerusalem in 70 AD, it was also in fulfilment of prophecy given by Jesus years before. For example, Matthew 24:1-2 tells us:

"Then Jesus went out and departed from the temple, and His disciples came up to show Him the buildings of the temple. And Jesus said to them, "Do you not see all these things? Assuredly, I say to you, not one stone shall be left here upon another, that shall not be thrown down." (Matt. 24:1-2). He said in addition: "But when you see Jerusalem surrounded by armies, then know that its desolation is near. Then let those who are in Judea flee to the mountains, let those who are in the midst of her depart, and let not

---

[15] Matthew Henry's Commentary, In One Volume, Zondervan.

those who are in the country enter her. For these are the days of vengeance, that all things which are written may be fulfilled." (Luke 21:20-22).

As told by Josephus Flavius, a Jewish historian who befriended the Romans and was an eyewitness to the city's destruction, several years before the city was destroyed God sent messengers to warn of its impending doom, and when the Jews disbelieved and put them in prison, like they did the prophets of old which God had sent to them before the city's first destruction, who, in addition to imprisonment, were often stoned or otherwise murdered, God sent signs in the heavens to warn them of its downfall. These things show His great mercy and forbearance, and His willingness that no one should perish but that all should come to repentance and be saved (2 Pet. 3:9).

Josephus gives us a startling view of the warnings that God sent to the people of Jerusalem prior to its destruction. For example:

In 66 AD, four years before it was destroyed, when the city was enjoying peace and prosperity, a star resembling a sword in the shape of a cross hung over the city at night, and a comet was seen in the sky for over a year. There was also the strange appearance of chariots and armed battalions hurtling through the sky at sunset. These manifestations continued for some time until they were seen by all of the city's inhabitants.[16]

The Roman historian, Cornelius Tacitus, testified of the signs:

"There were many prodigies presignifying their [the people of Jerusalem] ruin which was not averted by all the sacrifices and

---

[16] https://www.patheos.com/blogs/keithgiles/2018/02/7-signs-josephus-reveal-end-times-destruction/.

vows of that people. Armies were seen fighting in the air with brandished weapons. A fire fell upon the Temple from the clouds. The doors of the Temple were suddenly opened."

The Roman commander Titus is reported to have said:

"We have certainly had God for our assistant in this war, and it was no other than God who ejected the Jews out of these fortifications; for what could the hands of men, or any machines, do towards overthrowing these towers!"[17]

The destruction of Jerusalem by the Romans was the end of the Jewish Age. The temple was destroyed, and no longer did the priests offer sacrifices of sheep and oxen on the holy altar.[18]

God's judgement on Jerusalem shows not only what He is capable of, but the means by which He typically carries out His out His purposes - the armies of man.

Verses About God's Wrath

The following verses are among those that testify of God's wrath. In reading them, let us not forget that Scripture cannot be broken (John 10:35) and that all will come to pass.

"Vengeance is Mine, I will repay." - Deut. 32:35, Rom. 12:19.

"The Lord is a jealous and avenging God; the Lord is avenging and wrathful; the Lord takes vengeance on his adversaries and keeps wrath for his enemies." - Nah. 1:2-6.

---

[17] Ibid.

[18] https://bible.org/question/when-did-animal-sacrifices-stop-and-why.

"I will execute great vengeance on them with furious rebukes; and they shall know that I am the Lord, when I lay My vengeance upon them." - Ezek. 25:17.

"You shall break them with a rod of iron; You shall dash them to pieces like a potter's vessel'." - Ps. 2:9.

"Let no one deceive you with empty words, for because of these things the wrath of God comes upon the sons of disobedience." - Eph. 5:6.

"There will be weeping and gnashing of teeth." - Matt. 25:14-30.

These verses compliment many of the parables that we will see in a later chapter that portray Jesus as more divine than human, with the authority to judge all mankind. They include the parable of the *Wise and Foolish Virgins*, the parable of the *Talents*, the parable of the *Ten Minas*, the parable of the *Wedding Feast*, the parable of the *Faithful Servant and the Evil Servant*, the parable of the *Rich Fool,* and the *Parable of the Dragnet.*

The Day of Judgement

No one is exempt from the Day of Judgment. All will be judged and sentenced for their conduct on earth, for God requires an account.

"I tell you, on the day of judgment people will give account for every careless word they speak, for by your words you will be justified, and by your words you will be condemned." - Matt. 12:36-37.

"For we must all appear before the judgment seat of Christ, so that each one may receive what is due for what he has done in the body, whether good or evil." - 2 Cor. 5:10.

There are many absolutes in the world – hot and cold, light and darkness, good and evil, truth and falsehood, love and hate, right and wrong, sacred and profane. Likewise, there is a heaven and a hell; but only one awaits each of us on Judgment Day.

As stated in the chapter on Division, decisions made in life affect a soul's eternal destiny. When guided by the conscience as the Master plays on the heart strings, they work for our betterment. However, an ignorance of God will be of no excuse on Judgment Day. As it is known in the courts of law, *Ignorantia legis neminem excusat*, which is Latin for "ignorance of the law excuses no one."

As discussed in the last chapter, each of us is endowed with a spirit, or soul, the exclusive property of God (Ezek.18:4), and it is He to whom we must present ourselves in the end. We don't own our souls, He does; we didn't give ourselves a soul, He did, and He takes it back when we die, but we determine where it goes.

The soul is our true unpretentious self, and Bible tells us that when we die, the soul departs to one of two places as determined by us – a place of malevolent torment, confusion and darkness, or a place eloquent of benevolent peace, joy and enlightenment.

On that fateful day, thrones will be set in place and books opened (Dan. 7:9, 2 Cor. 5:10), and souls will be judged for how they conducted themselves when in the body. Everything anyone has ever done or said is going to be brought to light and judged. In particular, judgement will be based on what they did about God and His Son. Heaven and earth will be witnesses against us (Matt. 12:41-42). An eternity of life will open for some, and an eternity of torment will open for others.

Did we, while in the world, acknowledge Him as Father, and Jesus Christ as His Son? Did we educate ourselves in the Word? Did we set our minds on things above, not on things that are on earth (Col. 3:2)? Did we thank Him for giving us the good things that supported and comforted our lives? Did we thank Him for the body He gave us? Did we thank Him for the air, food, water and health that we enjoyed?

"Whosoever shall deny Me before men, him shall I also deny before My Father who is in heaven." - Matt. 10:33.

Many people believe that they're intrinsically accountable to no one but themselves. Pride rules their hearts and separates them from God because their soul is not upright (Hab. 2:4, " Behold the proud, His soul is not upright."). Pride is the worst sin of the Bible because it is rebellion against God. God will not circumvent or countermand man's gift of free choice, but whatever a man sows that shall he also reap (Gal. 6:7). No one is exempt from that Day. We will be weighed in the balances by Jesus. The Day of Judgment will be to the ungodly like a burning furnace.

"For behold, the day is coming, burning like an oven, and all the proud, yes, all who do wickedly will be stubble. And the day which is coming shall burn them up," says the Lord of hosts."– Mal. 4:1.

"A day is coming when human pride will be ended and human arrogance destroyed. Then the Lord alone will be exalted." - Isa. 2:11.

"For all have sinned and come short of the glory of God." - Rom. 3:23.

Jesus knows our shortcomings and failures, and what our lives have been like, what troubles and worries and losses we've had, and how we have suffered. He knows how we've treated others of God's creation, who have just as much right to live and be treated with fairness as we have. Throughout His mission on earth, He emphasized that it is our intentions, our motivations, as well as our acts, that are going to be judged. This is profound truth. No religion is so severe as Christianity. It makes us fear the Lord.

"You have heard that it was said to those of old, 'You shall not murder, and whoever murders will be in danger of the judgment.' But I say to you that whoever is angry with his brother without a cause shall be in danger of the judgment." - Matt. 5:22.

I have been in a murdering mood more than once, especially when my hopes were dashed or my plans thwarted, or some bitter disappointment or unexpected defeat was experienced. I was often crushed, overwhelmed by the loss. At other times, I was furious and full of bitterness and resentment. I'm sure that what I felt in my heart during those times will count against me in the Judgement.

"For nothing is secret that will not be revealed, nor anything hidden that will not be known and come to light." - Luke 8:17.

Everything that man does is right in his own eyes, but the Lord weighs the spirit. God sees all and knows all; it is His Nature, as ours is knowing and understanding through our five senses and by the limited intellects which we have been given. He postpones His wrath only because He is longsuffering, not willing that anyone should perish, but that all should come to repentance.

"The Lord is not slack concerning His promise, as some count slackness, but is longsuffering toward us, not willing that any should perish but that all should come to repentance." - 2 Pet. 3:9.

If we sin, we can be washed clean by wholeheartedly turning to God and asking for His forgiveness. I, for one, am grateful that He postpones His wrath and allows me time to repent.

People who are beset with heart-rending troubles that they cannot understand are quick to blame God for them, and some hold a grudge against Him for the rest of their lives. However, it is a grave mistake, for we do not know all the purposes of God, and He is sovereign over everything.

"But now, O Lord, You are our Father; we are the clay, and You our potter; and we are all the work of Your hand." - Isa. 64:8.

When beset with a crushing defeat or loss, we should ask ourselves if it was orchestrated by God for some reason, perhaps for our tempering or correction. Doing this can lead to serious contemplation and prayer. God may not be behind the tragic events of our lives, but then again it is entirely possible that the events were arranged in accordance with His purposes.

We learned from the chapter on the Value of Suffering that we should consider all disappointments in life as opportunities in disguise and possible turning points, things that are sent to incite us to action or self-appraisal and reevaluation of the situation.

"And we know that all things work together for good to those who love God, to those who are the called according to His purpose." - Rom. 8:28.

The following parable illustrates God's wrath and forbearance, and of the opportunity given to us to become fruitful and productive.

The Parable of the Fruit Tree Taking Up Space in the Garden

"So he said to the man who took care of the vineyard, 'For three years now I've been coming to look for fruit on this fig tree and haven't found any. Cut it down! Why should it use up the soil?' "But he answered and said to him, 'Sir, let it alone this year also, until I dig around it and fertilize it. And if it bears fruit, well. But if not, after that you can cut it down.'" (Luke 13:7-9).

God is the owner. The gardener is Jesus, the one who takes cares of the tree, providing it with the living water and fertilizer of His Word.

But isn't Jesus God incarnate, essentially the same as God? How then can the owner and the gardener be separate personages in this parable? Perhaps, it is like when we argue with ourselves, as when we weigh the pros and cons of something, as when we are trying to solve a problem or determine the best course of action to pursue.

What the tree represents, whether it is Israel during the time of Jesus's earthly ministry or whether it is ourselves, is immaterial. God is seen to be the way He is depicted in many of the other parables – an authority that is capable of decisiveness and wrath.

Jesus, however, persists in dissuading the Lord by putting forth an alternative, knowing that no fruit can be produced on the tree without Him.

God is a Consuming Fire

"For behold, the Lord will come with fire and with His chariots, like a whirlwind, to render His anger with fury, and His rebuke with flames of fire." - Isa. 66:15.

Fear of God is reverence for Him. We are to fear God and keep His commandments (Lev. 19:14, Mal. 1:4-6, Eccl. 12:13, Matt. 10:28), for we are accountable to Him. However, as stated before, the fear of God is not being preached or otherwise taught today. It has gone out of style. We hear only of God's love and compassion. But God is very much to be feared, and fear of Him is what He expects of each of us, Christian and non-Christian alike.

"I could come into your midst and in one moment consume you." - Ex. 33:5.

Aaron's sons, Abihu and Nadab, were destroyed by fire when they offered strange fire, a profane sacrifice, in the tabernacle (Lev. 10:1-20). Their sacrifice was a sign of disregard for the holiness of God and the need to honor Him in holy fear.

Fire descended from above when Elijah confronted the prophets of Baal on Mount Carmel (1 Kings 18:20-40). It occurred after the prophets of Baal called upon their god all day to rain fire from heaven, but to no avail. It was then that Elijah built an altar of stones, dug a trench around it, put the sacrifice on the top of the wood, and called for water to be poured over the altar and the sacrifice three times. So the water ran all around the altar; and filled the trench with water. When Elijah called upon the Lord, the Lord sent fire from heaven that consumed the sacrifice, wood, stones, dust and even licked up the water that was in the trench. After that, the anger of the Lord turned towards the false prophets, and He ordered Elijah to capture and slay them, which he did.

"His eyes were like a flame of fire, and on His head were many crowns." - Rev. 19:12.

God's wrath on lawless and unrighteous man will executed

on the Day of Judgment when He separates the sheep from the goats, and vindicates the suffering inflicted on the poor and feeble innocents of the world and on the saints down through the ages.

"Then you shall again discern between the righteous and the wicked, between one who serves God and one who does not serve Him." – Mal. 3:18.

"It is a fearful thing to fall into the hands of the living God." - Heb. 10:31.

Armageddon, the last of all wars, will see fire will come down from heaven and devour the armies gathered against God (Rev. 20:9).

"For if God did not spare angels when they sinned, but sent them to hell putting them in chains of darkness to be held for judgment; if He did not spare the ancient world when He brought the flood on its ungodly people, but protected Noah, a preacher of righteousness, and seven others; if He condemned the cities of Sodom and Gomorrah by burning them to ashes, and made them an example of what is going to happen to the ungodly; and if He rescued Lot, a righteous man, who was distressed by the depraved conduct of the lawless (for that righteous man, living among them day after day, was tormented in his righteous soul by the lawless deeds he saw and heard) – if this is so, then the Lord knows how to rescue the godly from trials and to hold the unrighteous for punishment on the day of judgment." - 2 Pet. 2:4-9.

It is well to remember that God's Spirit is more than a spirit of love, mercy, forgiveness and compassion.

Satan's Objectives

Satan's primary objective has always been and is to draw people away from God. In recent times, he has been successful in doing it by getting people to adopt a self-gratification or living to the flesh philosophy (Rom. 8:12-13). His tools are deceit and deception, and they are employed remarkably well in radio, newspaper, television, the Internet and other forms of social media.

The rise of homosexuality and permissiveness in our culture, the negative effect it has on marriage and family, and the prolific drug culture that thrives in the big cities of the world and robs people of their productivity and self-respect, are typical examples of Satan's victories. Of course, wars which kill people before they have a chance to know God are highly effective in ruining souls too, and are nest beds for deceit and deception. People are easily swayed during times of war to dehumanize the enemy, as was exhibited in the extreme in Stalin's Russia and Hitler's Germany. The dehumanization caused the horrendous and futile waste of life in WWII. As Judgement Day approaches, and some say it is likely to occur before the end of this century, a day prefaced by Armageddon, the devil can be expected to work even harder than normal because he knows he hasn't much time left (Rev. 12:12).

Nevertheless, God says beforehand,

"O enemy, destructions are finished forever! And you have destroyed cities; even their memory has perished. But the Lord shall endure forever. He has prepared His throne for judgment. He shall judge the world in righteousness, and He shall administer judgment for the peoples in uprightness." - Ps. 9:6-8.

Before the Day of Judgement, there is going to be what is called the Day of the Lord, in which the elements of the earth will melt with fervent heat and be destroyed by fire. It is described in 2 Pet. 3:10-11. The two should not be confused, for both will take place to accomplish God's will against evil.

In Revelation 15:1-8, John witnessed great and amazing signs in heaven of God's coming wrath on mankind, including seven plagues that He is going to send to the earth.

What Many People Believe

The common belief of many people is that hell, if it exists at all, is only a holding place, something like a Purgatory, and that everyone goes to heaven eventually no matter how they conduct themselves on earth. They believe that all roads lead to heaven, and it doesn't matter what religion you happen to adhere to. Others believe they will be admitted to heaven by good works, and the more good works they do, such as being considerate of their fellowman and courteous to stranger, donating time and money to good causes and refraining from hurting others, the better.

They don't want to hear about God's wrath. They don't want to hear about sin and judgement. They don't want to hear about His stern side. They don't want to fear the Lord. As a result, the passages of Scripture that teach these things are seldom if ever preached; the pulpit is silent about them. However, the Bible is filled with them. Instead, most people expect and want, but for no good reason, His love, mercy, goodness and compassion.

Then there are those who believe that after death God will offer them a second chance at redemption. But the Bible says there are no second chances, but that today is the acceptable day of salvation (Isa. 55:6, 2 Cor. 6:2). If we do not take advantage of the day, we lose out for tomorrow. It is the way things are with God.

Many also believe that everyone will meet again in the next life, regardless of what they did on earth, and that they will be able to share their past experiences. But the Bible takes issue with this belief as well, and examples are legion. The Word tells us that there is only one way to gain admittance to heaven, and that is through the blood of Jesus Christ (Acts 4:12, John 6:54, John 5:24, John 14:6). It describes only two places where all souls will be sent – heaven and hell – and it says that there is a great gulf fixed between them so that no one from one place can visit any in the other (Luke 16:26).

Such mistaken beliefs are the result of wishful thinking based on a person's attempts at playing God, which is nothing but humanism. They are egocentric, not God-centric, beliefs.

There is a sort of Christian humanism today that ignores the stern side of God. The Bible teaches that toward the end of the age there will be times like this, there will be belief systems like this, and that it will increase in prevalence throughout the world. And that is what we are seeing. It teaches that scoffers will come in the last days. Cynics. People who say that God is not the God of the Bible, but a god of man's own invention. They will stop their ears to the truth and seek out messages and doctrines that condone their lifestyles. They will raise up teachers who will tell them what their itching ears want to hear (2 Tim. 4:3). The gift of free will has become license to believe whatever people want to believe. Scripture tells us, however, that they are deceived by the power of Satan.

"Whose minds the god of this age has blinded, who do not believe, lest the light of the gospel of the glory of Christ, who is the image of God, should shine on them." - 2 Cor. 4:4.

God warned man that if he rebelled against Him he would die, and man has been suffering and dying ever since. He tells us in His Word that He will avenge those who treat others mercilessly, and He is going to do it.

Let no one doubt that God is a God of wrath, a mighty Man (Isa. 42:13) who is opposed to evil. He will punish those who ignore His warnings and disobey His Word.

"I will punish the world for its evil, and the wicked for their iniquity; I will put an end to the pomp of the arrogant, and lay low the pompous pride of the ruthless." - Isa. 13:11.

"He shall strike the earth with the rod of His mouth, and with the breath of His lips he shall kill the wicked. Righteousness shall be the belt of His waist, and faithfulness the belt of His loins." - Isa. 11:4-5.

Jesus died on the cross for all of humankind, and desires everyone in every generation to be saved (1 Tim. 2:4-6), but He did more than that. He told us in explicit terms what lies ahead. His coming changed everything by instituting a new type of division on earth – one based on good and evil, one never seen before or after Him. He united many people in a common cause based on a new truth that went against the status quo. The message of division is both direct and unequivocal, and we see evidences of it every day. It is a message like that of the winnowing fan, which, although seldom if ever preached, has vital significance for us all.

Soon He will return to gather and burn up the chaff of His field – the evil tares of every imperfect character – with the fire of retributive justice, and save the wheat, the good seeds that He has planted on the earth. It will be a weeding out of mankind, one more thorough than anything man could devise, for it will be determined by each and every person primarily based on belief in Him.

Chapter 6 Additional Signs of God's Displeasure

Throughout history, examples of God's apparent displeasure with man have been exhibited in various ways and forms. Some of them have already been discussed. What has not been discussed is that sometimes they seem to have included the weather.

"He loads the clouds with moisture; He scatters His lightning through them. At his direction they swirl around over the face of the whole earth to do whatever he commands them. He brings the clouds to punish people, or to water His earth and show His love." - Job 37:11-13.

"He causes the vapors to ascend from the ends of the earth; He makes lightning for the rain; He brings the wind out of His treasuries. - Ps. 135:7.

"Lightning and hail, snow and clouds, stormy winds that do his bidding." - Ps. 148:8.

Jesus commanded the winds and the waves, and they became calm, both bearing witness to Him (for example, Matt. 8:26-27).

Scientists tell us that storms form of themselves by the natural processes that are at work in the atmosphere; that the winds are caused primarily by air temperature and pressure gradients, which are differences in temperature or pressure in a volume of air. The gradients are primarily created by the daytime heating of the air and the ground by the Sun, and by the nighttime cooling of the air and ground in the absence of the Sun, and by lesser effects that will be discussed. In other words, they are primarily caused by the daily heating and cooling of the ground and the atmosphere. A contributing factor is the presence of water vapor (moisture) in the air. The varying amounts of water vapor in the atmosphere can change its temperature or pressure.

Rising water vapor cools with altitude, forms clouds and, as it condenses into larger droplets, it falls as rain. The rain, in turn, has a cooling effect on the air and the earth, as readily seen after a rain, and the cooling effect causes air temperature and pressure gradients that, in turn, cause winds. In fact, water vapor plays a larger role in the formation of the winds and weather than many people realize.

"The impacts of climate change and variability on the quality of human life occur primarily through changes in the water cycle."[19]

Trees and forests retain and absorb water but also transpire water into the atmosphere.[20] As the surface water evaporates, winds move water in the air from the sea to the land.

As the forests of the world are destroyed to make room for livestock and the crops that feed them, which is the major impetus for deforestation today, the plentiful source of water vapor that trees add to the atmosphere diminishes. As a result, the winds and the weather are greatly affected.

Do not underestimate the importance of trees. God used a tree to work the miracle of Marah through the hands of Moses, turning water unfit for drinking into palatable water (Ex. 15:23-25). He also used a tree for crucifying His only Son

---

[19] www.science.nasa.gov/earth-science/oceanography/ocean-earth-system/ocean-water-cycle.
[20] eschooltoday.com/learn/effects-of-deforestation/.

If deforestation continues at its present rate, as all signs indicate that it will, the contribution that trees and forests make to the amount of water vapor in the air will continue to decrease. In fact, deforestation is one of the primary causes of climate change and global warming.

"With half of all the earth's forests gone, and four million trees cut down each year just for paper use, the amount of carbon dioxide is rising. With more carbon dioxide in the atmosphere, more of the Sun's radiation is being reflected back to earth, instead of space, and this is causing our average temperature to rise. In this way, deforestation is a major issue when it comes to global warming."[21]

This rationally explains much of the weather we normally see. However, is weather always caused by natural processes, or influenced by something that man does?

Surely, the God who made all things can guide and govern them all, for the power that could make all things must certainly have power to guide and direct them. It is unwise to place limits on the capabilities of the Sovereign Lord.

"When He utters His voice, there is a multitude of waters in the heavens: and He causes the vapors to ascend from the ends of the earth. He makes lightning for the rain; He brings the wind out of His treasuries." - Jer. 10:13.

Many, like Martin Luther, believe that either God or the devil is behind severe weather; the problem is figuring out which one.

---

[21] www.nature.com/scitable/blog/green-science/deforestation_and_global.

Consider, for example, the severe winter weather that struck Europe during WWI, in Soviet Russia in the 1930s, and in all of Europe again during WWII. These were times of horrendous devastation and untold loss of life. Could it have been because to God's displeasure with man?

Also consider the Battle of Dunkirk in June 1940, when 400,000 British and French soldiers were trapped on the north coast of France at Dunkirk by the blitzkrieg unleashed by Germany against France and the low countries. The German forces were only 10 miles away and could easily have cornered the Allied troops. But thick fog and clouds settled over the beaches, and the English Channel became unusually calm, enabling British private flotillas of small boats to ferry the soldiers across to safety. The unusual weather lasted for nine days while the evacuation took place. The Allied army was preserved to fight another day. Winston Churchill called the evacuation of Dunkirk a miracle of deliverance.

We are now witnessing severe weather patterns that wreak havoc throughout the world with a greater frequency than in the past. These patterns are normally attributed to global warming. However, Jesus told us that there would be signs accompanying the end times, and that we could expect to see violent earthquakes and weather systems to occur, for the powers of the heavens will be shaken.

"And there will be signs in the Sun, in the Moon, and in the stars; and on the earth distress of nations, with perplexity, the sea and the waves roaring, men's hearts failing them from fear and the expectation of those things which are coming on the earth, for the powers of the heavens will be shaken." - Luke 21:25-26.

The next time you witness or hear about a freak or ferocious storm, ask yourself why it is happening.

Chapter 7 Hell

"And many of those who sleep in the dust of the earth shall awake, some to everlasting life, some to shame and everlasting contempt." - Dan. 12:2.

I've never heard anyone say, "I hope you go to heaven," or "Go to heaven!" But I've heard people use "hell" in that context many times. It is often used in vicious, derogatory ways because, even if people do not believe in the reality of hell, everyone associates pain and suffering with it.

But it is only by a right understanding of hell that we obtain a right understanding of the gospel and realize how people can end up in that forsaken place for eternity. We need never fear the Word of God, for it is provided for our reproof and instruction in righteousness (2 Tim. 3:16-17).

The word "hell" is derived from the Anglo-Saxon word "hellia," which itself is derived from the Hebrew Sheol or the three Greek words, Hades, Gehenna or Tartarus, which all mean either "unseen state" or abode of the damned in the afterlife.[22] [23] It is one of two places that God made for the future life. It is the banishment from all that is light, pleasant, joyous, peaceful and comfortable. It is the second death (Rev. 20:14). In the *Inferno*, Dante tells us that the sign extending above hell's portal reads: "Abandon all hope ye who enter here." Nothing is better than heaven, and nothing is worse than hell.

---

[22] https://www.britannica.com/topic/Gehenna.

[23] http://gochristianhelps.com/books/m/moser/hellfire.html.

The original concept of hell predates the Bible,[24] meaning that its truth was communicated to man perhaps as early as Adam, and from then on was passed to succeeding generations in one form or another.

Hell is eternal, which means it lasts forever and has no beginning or end. It exists now, has always existed, and will exist forever. Its chief occupants will be the devil and his fallen angels (Matt. 25:41), but it will be filled with the ungodly (Rev. 20:15).

Hell's Size and Fires

Hell must be immense (Isa. 5:15, Jude 1:6), but we do not know how large it is, or if it has various levels, as Dante Alighieri's books, *The Inferno*, *Purgatory* and *The Divine Comedy* suggest. It is called the bottomless pit in the Book of Revelation (Rev. 9: 11-12, 17:8, 20:1-15). So its dimensions are unknown.

Jesus talked about hell more than he did about heaven. He undoubtedly did so because He wants man to recognize and internalize hell's significance to our lives. It may also be because He knows that the more man is aware of its horrors, the more inclined he will be to do whatever is necessary to avoid it.

As discussed in the chapter on His Winnowing Fan, Jesus taught His disciples about hell in the parable of the *Wheat and the Tares.*

"As the tares are gathered and burned in the fire, so it will be at the end of this age. The Son of Man will send out His angels, and they will gather out of His kingdom all things that offend, and those

---

[24] Most scholars believe that the written Word began with the Book of Genesis which was given to Moses.

who practice lawlessness, and will cast them into the furnace of fire. There will be wailing and gnashing of teeth." - Matt. 13:36-42.

The message of the tares, like that of the winnowing fan and also of division, is direct and unequivocal. It cannot be misunderstood.

Heaven awaits the wheat, the good seeds that the Son of God planted in the world, and the vengeance of eternal fire awaits the tares that the devil planted.

Once again, we see the dichotomy between good and evil, right and wrong and truth and falsehood, that exists in the world. Once again, we see that they are absolute, not relative, terms and constitute as much a part of God's creation as light and darkness. There is simply no way of getting around it.

Some people are willing to accept the Bible's description of hell metaphorically but not literally. In fact, they claim that the Bible is a collection of stories that have little or nothing to do with reality. However, it is precisely because the Bible is the Word of God that it can be taken literally, and trusted implicitly. It is unlike any other book ever written. It challenges everyday thinking on every one of its pages. It was meant to be taken literally, for how else could anyone be sure of their salvation?

Regarding the flames of hell, the winnowing fan passage (Luke 3:17) tells us that it has unquenchable fire – fire that cannot be put out. The Book of Jude tells us that the tares of the world are reserved for the blackness of darkness forever (Jude 12:13).

Hell is described in the Book of Job as:

"The land of darkness and the shadow of death, a land as dark as darkness itself, as the shadow of death, without any order, where even the light is like darkness. - Job 10:21-22.

These passages indicate that the flames of hell are not what we are accustomed to, for they are dark not glowing flames, meaning that they give off heat but no light. Is such a thing possible in the world in which we live?

It turns out that such a thing is possible. Flames can be dark and at the same time give off extreme heat. For example, by heating a gas called a plasma, which is a gas of ions and free electrons, to very high temperatures like those found in controlled thermal fusion reactors, like the Russian Tokamak, a plasma can be extremely hot but dark or invisible.[25] It is because plasma, the fourth state of matter, can exist in three forms: dark, glow and arc, but visible light is emitted only in the glow and arc modes – examples of which are lightening, the auroras, fluorescent light tubes and a rocket's exhaust. Visible light is not emitted in the dark mode. Therefore, since natural laws apply to all that God has created, excruciating fire and the blackness of darkness forever awaits the tares of this world.

What can oppose His purposes? Who can usurp His sovereignty? Who can challenge His righteousness? What can dim His eyes?

"Who can say to Him, what are You doing?" - Job. 9:12.

The Justice of Sentencing Souls to Hell

Many question the fairness of condemning people to hell for any reason, and particularly for not believing in Jesus Christ. They do not understand how a God of love, mercy and compassion could

---

[25] https://physics.stackexchange.com/questions/445571/.Ibid.

do such things. They do not understand that the God of love, mercy and compassion is also the God of holiness, righteousness and judgment, that He hates evil, and the reason for the misunderstanding is that they are not familiar with the Word of God.

"The Lord looks down from heaven upon the children of men, to see if there are any who understand, who seek God." - Ps. 14:2.

Because many are unfamiliar with God's Word, they choose to ignore the stern side of God, and focus only on His genial side. They don't want to hear about justice, only mercy. They don't want to hear about sin. They have no room in their lives for His commandments and admonitions. So they cast the Bible, God and Jesus aside to pursue their luxuries and selfish desires. They may be Christians in the sense that Western civilization is Christian, but if they have a Bible at home it is left to collect dust on the shelf.

The Bible is very clear about many things. It tells us that Jesus created all things (John 1:3), that in Him all things consist (Col. 1:16-17) and that He has authority over heaven and earth (John 5:22-29, Matt. 28:18). He told the people that legions of angels were at His command, and that He will judge all souls. But the most remarkable thing about Jesus is that He not only claimed that He was God, but He is God (for example, John 1:1-4, John 10:30, John 11:25-26).

The living Jesus remains the most neglected person ever to live. He lives in the Scriptures in both the Old and New Testaments. He is seated at the right hand of God (Acts 7:55-56, 1 Pet. 3:22, Rom. 8:34). He came to earth in the form of a man to do all the things He said He would do – preach the kingdom of God, separate the chaff from the wheat and save those who are lost.

They are three distinct purposes that no one should be confused about. However, those who do not hear or read the Word of God never hear about them or never hear about all of them, nor do they understand them, and nor do they know Him.

Man's eternal destination of heaven or hell is a doctrine of the church called predestination. It is part of God's eternal purpose for man. However, many people, including Christians, struggle with it, and for that reason alone it is discussed throughout this book in the hopes that it may become clear.

Hell is a place of defilement. One must be unwashed of their sins to enter its gates. The murderer, the sexually immoral, the whoremonger, the homosexual, the sodomite, the sorcerer, the idolater, the thief, the covetous, the drunkard, the reviler, the extortioner, all liars, and all others who offend God and are at enmity with Him will be locked out of heaven and have their part in the lake of fire (1 Cor. 6:9, Rev. 21:8).

As discussed in the chapter on Division, one of God's great purposes is to populate heaven and hell, and, from the looks of things both past and present, He wants a full house in both of them before it is all over.

Hell's Location

Hell is revealed in Scripture as located beneath the earth. For example, Ephesians 4:9 states that it is in the lower parts of the earth, and Revelation 20:1 describes it as a bottomless pit. For those who believe the earth to be flat instead of round, which is entirely consistent with Scripture since it never suggests or implies anything to the contrary, the location of hell is "down," towards the great deep. The world described in the Bible is built upon the waters of the great deep, whose foundations can never to be discovered by man, as written in the Book of Jeremiah:

"Thus says the Lord, who gives the Sun for a light by day, the ordinances of the Moon and the stars for a light by night, who disturbs the sea, and its waves roar (the Lord of hosts is His name): if those ordinances depart from before Me, says the Lord, then the seed of Israel shall also cease from being a nation before Me forever. Only if the heavens above can be measured and the foundations of the earth below be searched out will I reject all the descendants of Israel because of all they have done, declares the Lord." - Jer. 31:35-37.

God is telling us in this passage that if it were it possible for the Sun, Moon and stars to vanish from His sight, and if it were possible to measure the heavens above or search out the foundations of the earth below, then He would forsake all the seed of Israel.

Since God will never cast off all the seed of Israel, as affirmed throughout the Holy Scriptures, man will never be able to measure the heavens above or search out the foundations of the earth below.

Very little is known directly about the interior of the earth. The deepest hole ever drilled into the earth, the Kola well, is only 7.61 miles (12.2 km).[26] which is barely a fourth of the thickness of the earth's crust, the outermost layer of the earth.[27] Therefore, scientists must depend on theories and educated guesses based

---

[26] https://en.wikipedia.org/wiki/Kola_Superdeep_Borehole.

[27] From analysis of seismic waves sent through the earth, the earth's crust is determined to extend about 30 miles beneath the continents, and about 3-6 miles beneath the ocean floors. Below the crust is the mantle, which is composed denser rock. (Ref. hthttps://www.britannica.com/place/Earth/The-outer-shell.

on seismological data to explain what lies below the surface of the earth. Scientists claim that the earth has a molten iron core.[28]

Men have known for years that the lower you go in mines, the greater the temperature. Using seismological data, scientists have estimated that the temperature of the earth's iron core is about 9,800° F, which is based on laboratory experiments that simulate the theorized high pressures and temperatures that are assumed to exist.[29] [30] This information tends to support the Bible's description of hell as a place of intense heat.

Hell is the gigantic furnace prison underworld in which no escape is possible. Excruciating death without end! How horrible! We'll never be able imagine the ghastly and ceaseless agony of hell, nor can we imagine the unbelievable bliss of eternal life in heaven, but we can piece together some of its particulars by turning to Scripture.

Particulars About Hell

The following Scripture verses describe some of the particulars about hell:

"They have no rest day or night." - Rev. 14:11.

"Their worm does not die, and the fire is not quenched." - Mark 9:46, Isa. 66:24.

In both texts, the Hebrew word translated as "worm" literally

---

[28] http://www.bbc.com/earth/story/20150814-what-is-at-the-centre-of-earth.

[29] https://www.sciencedaily.com › releases › 2017/03.

[30] http://en.wikipedia.org/wiki/Earth's_inner_core.

means "maggot."[31] Those in hell are given a maggot that will not die, to torment them forever.

"He himself shall also drink of the wine of the wrath of God, which is poured out full strength into the cup of His indignation. He shall be tormented with fire and brimstone in the presence of the holy angels and in the presence of the Lamb. And the smoke of their torment ascends forever and ever; and they have no rest day or night." - Rev. 14:10-11.

"I am tormented in their flame." - Luke 16:24.

Fire speaks of judgement. Hell is the lake of fire and brimstone (sulfur), the fiery furnace of torment and doom that awaits evil souls on Judgement Day.

We see in these verses symbols of the agencies that God employs in His work of righteous retribution, those of perpetual unrest, fire and maggots, tangible suffering that lies in store for those who refuse His mercy and forgiveness, a choice freely given to humankind.

Christ warned that hell is so awful that it is better to cut off the hand or pluck out the eye that causes you to sin than to end up there (Matt.5:29-30).

Consider it well. Is there a more fitting judgement than hell for those who have contemptuously treated others, especially in heartless and cruel ways, and who have turned their backs on God and His Son? For God has foreseen from the foundation of the world the eternal destination of those who would and would not be His.

---

[31] https://www.gotquestions.org/worm-will-not-die.html.

The closest I can come to imagining what eternal punishment would be like is taken from stories of Mythology, such as that of Prometheus, who was chained to a rock on the side of a mountain where an eagle would come and peck out his liver every night. The liver would grow back during the day so the torture could be repeated forever. Or Sisyphus, who was condemned to push a heavy boulder up a hill with both hands. However, every time when he was about to roll it over the crest, the weight forced it back down the hill, so that he was forced to push it up again for eternity. (Homer, *Odyssey, Book 11*).

As we have seen, God has appointed darkness and excruciating fire for the punishment of those who have ignored or turned their back on Him and treated His sheep with arrogance, cruelty and injustice.

"For behold, the day is coming, burning like an oven, and all the proud, yes, all who do wickedly will be stubble. And the day which is coming shall burn them up," says the Lord of hosts."– Mal. 4:1.

How shall we escape so great a punishment? The answer is by obeying Him who gave us life, who holds our every breath in His hands (Dan. 5:23, Job. 12:10, Acts 17:25).

The default destination of all souls is hell (John 3:18). But God offers the way out through His Son, Jesus Christ. He's the Savior who gives us salvation, nor is there salvation in any other (Acts 4:12, John 14:6). The unrivaled gift was first announced by the Prophets and later by the Lord, Himself, and confirmed through His Word and by those who heard Him, God also bearing witness with signs and wonders and gifts of the Holy Spirit (Heb. 2:3-4). One needs only to reach out and take hold of it (2 Cor, 9:15, Rom. 5:15 and 5:17) to have their eternal destiny changed to the kingdom of God. But for many, many people, it is a very difficult thing to do because it means forfeiting their pride to God, and few ever find it in themselves to do it.

"Enter by the narrow gate; for wide is the gate and broad is the way that leads to destruction, and there are many who go in by it. Because narrow is the gate and difficult is the way which leads to life, and there are few who find it." - Matt. 7:13-14.

Nevertheless, if we do nothing, then assuredly we will find ourselves in that terrible place of torment.

"Your hand will find all Your enemies; Your right hand will find those who hate You. You shall make them as a fiery oven in the time of Your anger. The Lord shall swallow them up in His wrath, and the fire shall devour them." - Ps. 21:8-9.

"When the wicked spring up like grass, and when all the workers of iniquity flourish, it is that they may be destroyed forever." - Ps. 92:7.

"Every plant which My heavenly Father has not planted will be uprooted." - Matt. 15:13.

"Anyone not found written in the Book of Life was cast into the lake of fire." - Rev. 20:15.

After knowing about the horrors of the underworld, wishing or telling someone to go is an uncaring act of villainy.

Chapter 8 The Spirit of God

"And the Spirit of God was hovering over the face of the waters." - Gen 1:2.

The Person and work of the Holy Spirit, the inspiring Spirit of God, is the subject of this chapter. The Spirit works in the world to restrain the powers of darkness from taking over the world. It is important to understand the restraining purpose as it is important to understand the purpose of division discussed in chapter 4, for they work together to accomplish God's will.

The Spirit of God is truth (1 John 5::6, John 14:26, John 15:26). He searches all things, even the things of God (1 Cor. 2:10-11). He gives us power and makes us bold to preach the Word (2 Tim. 1:7). He is our source of wisdom and revelation (Eph. 1:17-20). He is our helper (the Comforter in KJV). He helps us in our weaknesses, for we do not know what we should pray for as we ought, but the Spirit Himself makes intercession for us with groanings which cannot be uttered. God can give exceptional skill in wisdom, in knowledge and in all manner of workmanship to people through His Spirit (for example, Ex. 31:3). But the Holy Spirit is more than just an agent of God sent to do His will. He is more than an influence. He is a mighty Person and co-equal with God the Father and God the Son (1 John 5:7-8, NKJV).

The Work of the Holy Spirit in the World

The Spirit of God restrains the Satanic powers of evil from taking over the world in three ways – by convicting the world of sin, and of righteousness and of judgement (John 16:8-11, 2 Thess. 2:6-7). It is also accomplished through His work in the body of Christ.

The work of the Spirit will continue until He has done all that He can to save us. Then He will be taken out of the world. We do not know when that time will come, but some say it will be at the time of the rapture, when the trumpet of God loudly sounds throughout the world and believers in Christ rise to meet Him in the air (1 Thess. 4:16). Others believe it will be after the Great Tribulation (Rev. 7:14) and immediately before Christ returns to the earth as King of Kings and Lord of Lords (Rev. 19:16). But the moment when the Spirit departs, nothing will be left to restrain the powers of evil from taking over the world, and the earth will be turned into a living hell.

Jesus has been baptizing people with the Holy Spirit for 2000 years. He will come again to baptize not with the water of the living Word that is conducive to repentance, but with fire for vengeance as prophesized by John the Baptist (Matt. 3:11).

Man becomes a son of God, or a child of God, only by an act of will carried out by the Holy Spirit, as implicitly understood from John 6:44. One of the purposes of Christ, His redemptive purpose, is to turn man from his depravity and the power of Satan to the light of the truth of the Gospel of God that he may receive forgiveness of sins and be sanctified to God by faith, for God seeks those to worship Him in spirit and in truth (John. 4:24).

It is what the Holy Spirit does on His own and what He does through us that restrains evil from taking control of the world in its many insidious ways. How we assist the effort is mainly dependent on our faith, but it also depends on our ability to notice the ways of evil in the world. Evil people have evil motives and bear evil fruit. It is because the Holy Spirit is greater than he who is in the world (1 John 4:4), and gives us the knowledge we need to differentiate between good and evil, that the powers of evil are restrained.

Jesus taught us not to judge, but Christians are perhaps the most able to discern the difference between good and evil. The natural man, being full of evil himself, cannot often distinguish right from wrong, or good from evil, but Christians can.

The inspiration to read, plan and find solutions to the problems we face in life comes in part from the Holy Spirit. So does Scriptural insight and revelations about God. The Spirit is *unlimited*, in power and influence, as God is unlimited, and there is really nothing He cannot do, for with God all things are possible (Matt. 19:26).

Revivals are due to the Spirit of God. They are a stirring of God, a moving of the Spirit throughout the land.

The baptism of the Holy Spirit can cause people to speak in tongues, or different languages, and sometimes in a strange language of unknown origin, perhaps some being languages of heaven. They seem to do this while in a trance, which is the Spirit taking control of an individual for a period of time. It is in a trance where visions of God come to them (Num. 24:2-3, 1 Sam. 19:19-24).

Peter was put in a trance while in Joppa (Acts 10:9-23). He was on the housetop praying when he fell into a trance. He was to be sent by God to Gentiles to preach the Word, but as a Jew he had never dealt with Gentiles, so the Spirit gave him a vision of a giant white sheet being let down from heaven with all kinds of four-footed animals, birds and creeping things that were unclean for Jews to eat. It was done three times, and each time a voice came to him to rise, kill and eat, followed by "What God has cleansed you must not call common." As soon as the vision was taken away, the men who had been sent by Cornelius to ask him to come and preach the Word to them were at the door. Peter then realized that God wanted him to visit Gentiles and tell them about Jesus.

Daniel was in put in a trance by the Spirit when Gabriel spoke to him (Dan. 8:18), and again when he saw the night visions (Dan. 7:9).

Ezekiel was put in a trance when the Spirit lifted him up between earth and heaven and brought him "in the visions of God" to Jerusalem, to the entrance of the north gate of the inner court. (Ezek. 8:1-3).

As revealed in Acts 22:17-21, Paul was put into a trance when he returned to Jerusalem and was praying in the temple, and in the trance he saw Jesus saying to him, "Make haste, and get out of Jerusalem quickly, because they will not accept your testimony about Me."

In 2 Cor. 12:1-4, it is obvious that Paul was in a trance when he was caught up by the Spirit into the third heaven and heard words too that are too holy for man to repeat. A person can experience something so awesome that they're speechless when it comes to mind. Verse 1 implies that both visions and revelations of the Lord come from the Spirit.

John was ushered into the throne room of God by the Spirit and saw Him who looked like a jasper and a sardius stone in appearance, and there was a rainbow around the throne like an emerald, and from the throne proceeded lightnings, thunderings, and voices (Revelation 4:1-5).

The nine gifts of the Spirit are given in 1 Corinthians:

"For to one is given the word of wisdom through the Spirit, to another the word of knowledge through the same Spirit, to another faith by the same Spirit, to another gifts of healings by the same Spirit, to another the working of miracles, to another prophecy, to another discerning of spirits, to another different kinds of tongues, to another the interpretation of tongues. But one and the same Spirit works all these things, distributing to each one individually as He wills." - 1 Cor. 12:8-11.

Second Timothy tells us to "fan into flame the gift of God." (2 Tim. 1:6.)

The fruit of the Spirit is given in Galatians as follows:

"But the fruit of the Spirit is love, joy, peace, longsuffering, kindness, goodness, faithfulness, gentleness, self-control. Against such there is no law." - Gal. 5:22-23.

It is the Spirit of God who knocks on the door of our hearts and wants us to open so He can come in. It is the Spirit of God who accomplishes the wonderous work of God in the life of every baptized believer.

Nothing is more vital or precious than the Holy Spirit. He is the vitality of the living God, the fire of His soul, the substance of His being. He is never to be slighted or held in derision. All of life is because of the Spirit. That is why blasphemy of the Holy Spirit is called the unpardonable sin. Jesus severely warns in Mark 3:28-29:

"Assuredly, I say to you, all sins will be forgiven the sons of men, and whatever blasphemies they may utter; but he who blasphemes against the Holy Spirit never has forgiveness, but is subject to eternal condemnation." - Mark 3:28-29.

We do not know all that the Spirit of God does since, like God, He is omniscient, omnipotent and omnipresent, but it is certain that He moves in the hearts and lives of men and women, and is sure to do so until He is taken out of the world.

Man has been heralded as God's crowning achievement. He is marvelously and wonderfully made. Perhaps the most marvelous and wonderful thing about him is his capacity to receive the Word of God. Certainly, the sublimest of all miracles is how a human being can love God. It is effected by nothing short of the supernatural power of the Holy Spirit.

"You, however, are not in the realm of the flesh but are in the realm of the Spirit, if indeed the Spirit of God lives in you." - Rom. 8:9.

Man in his natural state is carnally minded and living at the behest of the evil one. But repentant man is a child of God. Moreover, the more a person abides in His Word, the more supernatural and less natural they become, for it is by the Spirit of the Lord who abides in them that divine truth is revealed.

Temples

A temple is a place of worship. The Jewish temple of the Bible no longer exists, for it was destroyed along with Jerusalem by the Romans under Titus Caesar in 70 AD, and it was never rebuilt.

Churches where the redeemed gather for communion and fellowship are earthly temples. The body of Christ, also referred to as the church, is, however, actually a collection of temples of the Holy Spirit (1 Cor. 6:19). Upon conversion and baptism, the Holy Spirit is given to a Christian and they become its dwelling place, the spiritual abode of the living God (2 Corinthians 6:16, Eph. 2:21).

A holy God will have a holy dwelling place. Whoever is in Christ is born again (1 John 5:1, John 3:3); they are a new creation (2 Cor. 5:17), having a new nature given them by God, a spiritual nature, making them more divinely supernatural than natural, more a part of God than they were before.

Other religions of the world, such as Buddhism and Taoism, have earthly temples, some of them elaborate, multitiered buildings stretching high in the sky. Some of their statues are covered with gold. Muslim temples are called mosques. Hindu temples are called mandirs. Jewish temples are called synagogues. They testify of the fact that every country, every race, every family and every individual has tried to explain the Great Being behind the world/universe/cosmos. But none have supernatural temples as does Christianity.

The fact that God is spirit (John 4:24) is said to be one of the sublimest truths ever presented to man, for He may be worshiped in any place.

The Trinity

For centuries, the doctrine that God is three Persons in One, or co-exists in three Persons, has been one of the principles of the Church even though its scriptural basis is not as solid as many would prefer. For example, the word "Trinity" is not found in Scripture. We see, however, that the concept is in Scripture.

The most concise passage of Scripture that describes the Trinity is 1 John 5: 7-8, but it is given in two versions of the Bible, the

King James Version and the New King James Version. Both versions say practically the same thing, which is:

"For there are three that bear witness in heaven: the Father, the Word, and the Holy Spirit; and these three are one." - 1 John 5: 7-8 (NKJV).

Other versions of the Bible translate the passage differently because they use different Greek texts from those used by the KJV and NKJV. For example, the NIV and ESV, respectively, state very similarly with only minor differences between them:

"For there are three that testify: the Spirit, the water and the blood; and the three are in agreement." - 1 John 5: 7-8 (NIV and ESV).

These two translations, as well as other new translations, say nothing about God being three persons.

Nevertheless, the concept of the Trinity has Scriptural basis. First, there are the passages that tell us there is only one God:

"Hear, O Israel: The Lord our God, the Lord is one!" (Deut. 6:4). "There is no other God but one." (1 Cor. 8:4), "God is one." (Gal. 3:20), and "There is one God and one Mediator between God and men, the Man Christ Jesus." (1 Tim. 2:5).

Secondly, the reality that God is more than one person is reflected in the Book of Genesis when the plural form of His name is given. For example, in Gen. 1:26 it says, "Then God said, "Let Us make man in Our image, according to Our likeness; let them have dominion over the fish of the sea, over the birds of the air, and over the cattle, over all the earth and over every creeping thing that creeps on the earth.""

Likewise, in Genesis 3:22: "Then the Lord God said, "Behold, the man has become like one of Us, to know good and evil." Genesis 11:7: "Come, let Us go down and there confuse their language, that they may not understand one another's speech." In Isaiah 6:8, God says, "Whom shall I send, and who will go for Us?" In each case, the pronoun "us" in the Hebrew is "Elohim," a plural form that definitely refers to more than two.32

John Chapter 1 says:

"And the Word was with God, and the Word was God. He was in the beginning with God. All things were made through Him, and without Him nothing was made that was made. In Him was life, and the life was the light of men." - John 1:1-4.

The truth of this verse, that God the Son created life, and in Him was life, distinguishes Jesus Christ from all other reformers. It exalts Him to the lofty supernatural heights of God and equates Him with God the Father.

Jesus said that He and His Father were one and that the Father was in the Him and He in the Father (John 10:30-39). By implication, since God is Spirit (John 4:24), it tells us that God is three Persons in One. Therefore, the doctrine of the Trinity is found in the New Testament.

The concept of the Holy Trinity is similar to "I am the Way, the Truth and the Life." (John 14:16). God consists of three Persons, but there is only one God. It is a majestic mystery in and of itself as well as a profundity that is beyond our capability to fully understand.

---

[32] https://www.gotquestions.org/Trinity-Bible.html.

There is a profound sense of loneliness about God (e.g., Jer. 2:4 and 3:19-20). You can almost feel sorry for Him, for there is no one like Him, no one to whom He can relate. He looks, therefore, to us, His creation, to acknowledge Him, and return His love. While other creatures obey and, because they obey, must respect Him, only man can return His love.

The Soul and Spirit of Man

The Bible uses both of the terms, soul and spirit. Is there a difference? There seems to be little, if any, difference. Some assume they are the same, but the Bible indicates, in Hebrews 4:12, that they are different, although not by much. "For the word of God is quick and powerful, and sharper than any two-edged sword, piercing even to the dividing asunder of soul and spirit, and of the joints and marrow, and is a discerner of the thoughts and intents of the heart."

Moses Gbenu states in *Back to Hell:*

"I believe a man has not profitably read the Bible until he gets to that point when the Bible begins to read him – until it begins to expose the reader and pierce the heart; until it begins to divide the soul and spirit of the reader; until it begins to divide the man's real heart-cry from the gambit of philosophy and humanistic psychology."

Similarly, the body and soul of man are bound together in a way that makes them practically inseparable. This is why the seventeenth century theologian, Father Martin Von Cochem, who having had discussions with people who had been raised from the dead, said in his book, *The Four Last Things: Death, Judgement, Hell, Heaven*, that death is a very painful experience since it is when the soul must depart from the body.

Matthew Henry, in his commentary,[33] said that believers are given a measure of the Holy Spirit somewhat as in a vessel of water, but that Christ was given the Spirit without measure, as in a fountain or a bottomless ocean. The agony at losing the Spirit that Jesus experienced when he died on the Cross must have been excruciating, as is evidenced by His loud cry right before He gave up His spirit (Matt. 27:50).

The remarkable transformation that occurs in a person "dead in trespasses and sins," which allows them to hear and respond to the gospel, is a work of the Holy Spirit.

More specifically, "No one can say that Jesus is Lord except by the Holy Spirit." (1 Cor. 12:3).

We do much to ensure the needs of the soul are well provided for by taking time out of our busy schedules to read the Word of God. The soul also receives nourishment when we pray to God. It is important to pray often, as the apostle Paul tells us, but it is also important to engage in contemplative prayer, a form of prayer that is perhaps best described in William Meninger's, *The Loving Search for God.* Remember that an army cannot march on an empty stomach, and the soul must be adequately nourished for spiritual warfare.

Brother Lawrence, in his book, *The Practice of the Presence of God,* says that when we give attention to the Creator, God comes to us in the secret place of the soul. That is a very profound statement. God, who is infinitely perfect in every Divine attribute, including holiness, grace, truth, power, knowledge and love, deigns to have fellowship with redeemed sinners who worship in

---

[33] Matthew Henry's Commentary, In One Volume, Zondervan.

spirit and in truth, but who are nevertheless full of imperfections and sins. However, it is in weakness that we find strength in Him.

Many people believe that Nature and God are synonymous, that God is in the rocks, the trees and in all living things. It is a belief that is fostered by pantheism or deism. But the Bible reveals that God resides in heaven ("Our Father, who is in heaven…").

St. John of the Cross, who is considered by many to be one of the most insightful of the saints, stated, "God sustains every soul and dwells in it substantially, even though it may be that of the greatest sinner in the world. This union between God and creatures always exists. By it, He conserves their being so that if the union should end they would immediately be annihilated and cease to exist." - St. John of the Cross, Book 2, Chapter 5, *The Ascent of Mount Carmel.*

While God and creation are distinct from one another, all of creation is sustained by God. I think of God's sustaining power in the breath of life He gives to all creatures, which we have until we die, and in His power to keep the atoms of all molecules from imploding into themselves by the electrical attraction the electrons have for the oppositely charged protons in the nucleus. Many physicists have been searching intently for this mysterious power, or force, for years, but to no avail.

The apostle Paul, speaking in the Areopagus in Athens, said,

"And He has made from one blood every nation of men to dwell on all the face of the earth, and has determined their preappointed times and the boundaries of their dwellings, so that they should seek the Lord, in the hope that they might grope for Him and find Him, though He is not far from each one of us; for in Him we live and move and have our being." - Acts 17:26-28.

Chapter 9 Man's Condition Before a Holy God

Irrespective of suffering, sickness and disease, the Bible teaches that man's true condition before a holy God is one of abject wretchedness.

"You say, I am rich; I have acquired wealth and do not need a thing. But you do not realize that you are wretched, pitiful, poor, blind and naked." - Rev. 3:17.

Being rich in worldly goods leads to pride, and pride, self-pride, is the worst sin in the Bible. It was the original sin of Adam and Eve, when they were deceived through the deceitful cunning of Satan to think they could be like God. It can be found behind all lying, cheating, misrepresentation, deception and other sins. It makes one out to be better than others. Self-pride essentially proclaims equality with God. It is the reason behind the concept expressed numerous times in the Bible that whatever man does is right in his own eyes (Deut. 12:8, Judges 17:6, Prov. 21:2, Prov. 12:15, Prov. 20:12, Isa. 5:21, etc.). The impurity of our hearts and lives make the work of our hands, and all our offerings, unclean before God (Hag. 2:13-14). They are unclean by our corruptions. Though pure in our own eyes, it be not so before the Lord.

The Bible tells us to put to death whatever is earthly in us: sexual immorality, impurity, passion, evil desire, and covetousness, which is idolatry, because on account of these the wrath of God is coming (Col. 3:5-6).

The Bible teaches that man's true condition is one of total

depravity, that his spiritual condition is bankrupt, and his only true purpose in life is to satisfy his evil desires. He wants nothing to do with God. The fact that wickedness is prospering in the world, and that most people are ignorant of the Bible testify of these things. Man's treatment of his fellowman through uncaring and hostile acts, and his violent and wasteful treatment of the earth and its environment, also testify of these things.

God knows our condition. He knows who and what we are. He knows all about our desires and where we're headed, and He generally allows us to live how we think is best for us to live. However, it does not make what we do acceptable in His sight.

"Know therefore that God exacts from you less less than your iniquity deserves." - Job 11:6.

The Bible teaches that everything man does is tainted with sin, and that his sinfulness affects his mind, will and emotions. Sin destroys the inner harmony of a man's life. There is no one who does good, no not one (Ps. 14:3, Rom. 3:12). It teaches that all our righteous acts are like filthy rags before a holy God (Isaiah 64:6).

"What is man, that he could be pure? And he who is born of a woman, that he could be righteous… who is abominable and filthy, who drinks iniquity like water!" - Job 15:14.

"His [man's] heart is deceitful and dreadfully wicked, who can know it?" - Jer. 17:9.

Two things that every person must come to understand are the holiness of God and the sinfulness of man.

When man repents of his sins and comes to Christ by faith, his inner heart is purified of the desire for sin, and the reproach against God is taken away. It is the inner cleansing that John the Baptist and Jesus called the baptism of the Holy Spirit (Mark 1:8, Acts 2:1-4). Meanwhile, however, man's most stupendous and glorious achievements are marked with a temporal importance, for the best and grandest accomplishments of mortals lose their glory in time. But the more one knows God, the more the wonder and admiration of Him increases.

The Word of God has come into all the world, but all the world has not received it. The Bible says that the general state of man is without the fear of the Lord. This fact emphasizes again the need to preach the sermon of the winnowing fan. It needs to be heard, and heard often, for it puts the fear of the Lord back into cold and wanton hearts and minds where it ought to live forever.

"They have all turned aside; they have together become unprofitable; there is none who does good, no, not one…There is no fear of God before their eyes." - Rom. 3:12 and 3:17.

People are quick to deny their sins and quick to disguise them, for if their sins are found out, and the Bible says they will be (Num. 32:23), then they are more concerned about how it might tarnish their image than how it might offends God and others. But when a person turns to Christianity and hears the Word of God, and that person receives the living Word in his or her heart, and the Word begins to dwell in them, then he or she soon begins to see their wretchedness and the need to be forgiven. Then the veil that is cast over the mind (Isa. 25:7) is removed and we see sin for what it is – an evil in itself and a reproach against God.

"How great Thou art, how great Thou art,
Then sings my soul, My Savior God, to Thee;

How great Thou art, how great Thou art!"[34]

God looks on the heart for the motives of what man does. We may think highly of ourselves, but in God's view we are wretched. We may attain popularity and befriend the whole world, but be at enmity with God and have no peace in our hearts. Jesus said that a man may gain the whole world but lose his soul.

"For what will it profit a man if he gains the whole world, and loses his own soul? Or what will a man give in exchange for his soul?" - Mark 8:36-37.

"There is no peace," says the Lord, "for the wicked." (Isa. 48:22). This is not a statement of warning, but of fact, and it applies to every natural, unrepentant man.

It is by our own lust that we are led astray by the tempter (James 1:14). We are therefore to look for the causes of every sin chiefly in ourselves – in our passions, appetites and inclinations.

An ageless struggle wages between the forces of good and evil, right and wrong and light and darkness that seeks to win each of us over to its side. It is called spiritual warfare, and it is waged against man by the devil and his many accomplices. Man can do practically nothing on his own against the powers of evil. He needs God's help to fight against them.

For those who read or who hear the Word, God says: "The fear of the Lord is the beginning of wisdom, and the knowledge of the Holy One is understanding." (Prov. 9:10). For the vast majority of people, however, He says: "Hearing you will hear, and shall not

---

[34] From the Christian hymn, How Great Thou Art, written by Carl Gustav Boberg in 1885.

understand; and seeing you will see, and not perceive." (Acts 28:26).

The sorrowful matter has one happy conclusion. In our captivity to sin, God thinks good thoughts about us (Jer. 29:11). He holds out hope for our future, and provides it through Jesus Christ, who, at the appropriate time (Gal. 4:4-5), was sent into the world to redeem the world.

Those who are drawn to God by His Spirit and reconciled to God by the blood of His Son receive a full pardon for their sins and eternal life in the bargain. They become Abraham's seed and heirs according to the promise (Gal. 3:29), redeemed by the blood and washed from their sins.

We don't know all of what happened on the cross, but we do know that Jesus took the hell and judgment that you and I deserve and placed it on Himself. It caused Him to proclaim, in a loud voice, "My God, My God, what hast thou forsaken Me?" (Matt. 27:46, Mark 15:34, Ps. 22:1, Is. 53:4-5, Gal. 3:13) since in that terrible moment a cloud passed between Him and God for the first and only time in eternity, hiding Him in the shadow because of God's hatred of sin.

It is a by sovereign act of God that man is born again (John 1:12-13). If it weren't for His great mercy, none of us would ever rise above our wretchedness and we would die in our sins.

However, if man never uses his gift of free choice to receive the gift of forgiveness – if he never hears about his true condition before a Holy God – then he remains as he is: wretched, pitiful, poor, blind and naked in the sight of God.

"Look to the rock from which you were hewn." - Isa. 51:1.

Chapter 10 The Creation

"Be exalted, O God, above the heavens; let Your glory be above all the earth." – Ps. 57:11.

The creation account is given in the first Book of the Old Testament, the Book of Genesis, and it is the very first thing encountered when one begins reading the Bible.

"In the beginning God created the heavens and the earth." - Gen. 1:1.

In the beginning there was God. God was there before anything else. He created the heavens and the earth; they did not evolve into being. He created them by voice command, if you will, and it indicates, perhaps more than anything else, the awesomeness of God's power.

This chapter first presents the creation account in detail. It then provides some important insights.

Genesis Chapter 1 describes the creation of the world. Chapter 2 describes the creation of Adam and Eve. While Chapter 2 has much to offer the student of the Bible, it is not pertinent to this discussion. The origin of evil and the consequences and far-reaching implications for the human race, have already been discussed in this book.

The full creation account is provided below, as taken from the New King James Version (NKJV) of the Holy Bible, the version that is most often cited in this book. It most closely resembles the King James Version (KJV), which is known as the Authorized Version.

"In the beginning God created the heavens and the earth. The earth was without form, and void; and darkness was on the face of the deep. And the Spirit of God was hovering over the face of the waters." (Gen. 1:1-2).

"Then God said, 'Let there be light'; and there was light. And God saw the light, that it was good; and God divided the light from the darkness. God called the light day, and the darkness He called night. So the evening and the morning were the first day." (Gen. 1:3-5).

"Then God said, 'Let there be a firmament in the midst of the waters, and let it divide the waters from the waters.' Thus God made the firmament, and divided the waters which were under the firmament from the waters which were above the firmament; and it was so. And God called the firmament Heaven. So the evening and the morning were the second day." (Gen 1:6-8).

"Then God said, 'Let the waters under the heavens be gathered together into one place, and let the dry land appear,' and it was so. And God called the dry land earth, and the gathering together of the waters He called seas. And God saw that it was good. Then God said, 'Let the earth bring forth grass, the herb that yields seed, and the fruit tree that yields fruit according to its kind, whose seed is in itself, on the earth'; and it was so. And the earth brought forth grass, the herb that yields seed according to its kind, and the tree that yields fruit, whose seed is in itself according to its kind. And God saw that it was good. So the evening and the morning were the third day." (Gen. 1:9-13).

"Then God said, 'Let there be lights in the firmament of the heavens to divide the day from the night; and let them be for signs and seasons, and for days and years; and let them be for lights in the firmament of the heavens to give light on the earth'; and it was so. Then God made two great lights: the greater light to rule the day, and the lesser light to rule the night. He made the stars also. God set them in the firmament of the heavens to give light on the earth, and to rule over the day and over the night, and to divide the light from the darkness. And God saw that it was good. So the evening and the morning were the fourth day." (Gen. 1:14-19).

"Then God said, 'Let the waters abound with an abundance of living creatures, and let birds fly above the earth across the face of the firmament of the heavens.' So God created great sea creatures and every living thing that moves, with which the waters abounded, according to their kind, and every winged bird according to its kind. And God saw that it was good. And God blessed them, saying, 'Be fruitful and multiply, and fill the waters in the seas, and let birds multiply on the earth.' So the evening and the morning were the fifth day." (Gen. 1:20-23).

"Then God said, 'Let the earth bring forth the living creature according to its kind: cattle and creeping thing and beast of the earth, each according to its kind'; and it was so. And God made the beast of the earth according to its kind, cattle according to its kind, and everything that creeps on the earth according to its kind. And God saw that it was good." (Gen. 1:24-25).

"Then God said, 'Let Us make man in Our image, according to Our likeness; let them have dominion over the fish of the sea, over the birds of the air, and over the cattle, over all the earth and over every creeping thing that creeps on the earth.' So God created man in His own image; in the image of God He created him; male and female He created them. Then God blessed them, and God said to them, 'Be fruitful and multiply; fill the earth and subdue it; have dominion over the fish of the sea, over the birds of the air, and over every living thing that moves on the earth.' (Gen. 1:26-28).

"And God said, 'See, I have given you every herb that yields seed which is on the face of all the earth, and every tree whose fruit yields seed; to you it shall be for food. Also, to every beast of the earth, to every bird of the air, and to everything that creeps on the earth, in which there is life, I have given every green herb for food'; and it was so. Then God saw everything that He had made, and indeed it was very good. So the evening and the morning were the sixth day." (Gen. 1:29-31).

On the seventh day, God rested from all that He had made.

Insights

It is interesting to note some of the differences between the creation account given in Genesis and the accepted theories of modern science regarding the evolution of life on earth and the origin of the world and the cosmos.

The Bible teaches that the Sun, Moon and heavens were not formed by accident, but were created for aiding and supporting man on earth. The Sun provides heat and light, and the Moon and stars are for marking the days, months and seasons. These purposes are centered around man. They emphasize his importance to God, whereas orthodox science, by endorsing the theory of evolution, the theories of the origin of the earth, Sun, Moon, stars and solar system, denies the existence of God and denigrates man by claiming that he came from slime[35] and inhabits a planet of no particular importance that is hurtling aimlessly through space.

The creation account is in stark contrast to the theories of modern science. For example, the Sun, Moon and stars were all created

---

[35] https://www.wired.co.uk/article/slime-evolution-gene.

at the same time (on the fourth day), and the earth was created before the Sun, Moon and stars (on the third day), whereas modern science teaches that the earth and Moon were formed after the Sun and stars.[36]

Plants were created before the Sun, which is also contrary to the tenets of modern science.

Accepted theory teaches that everything on earth and in the heavens evolved, that man is no more unique or special than other life forms in ways that cannot be explained by, or attributed to, the processes involved in evolution. In other words, it teaches that everything on earth, in the heavens, and about man can be explained by evolution.

Accepted theory teaches that sea creatures came before plants and land creatures came before flying creatures, but the Bible says that sea creatures came after plants, and flying creatures preceded land creatures.

The creation account indicates that everything was created mature – mountains, rocks, trees, animals and man – all were created in a mature state. It strongly indicates that it is the case as well for the Sun, Moon, stars, planets, galaxies, nebulae, comets and so forth – everything that is seen and unseen in the world/cosmos/universe. All was made ready for man when he was created on the sixth day. The Garden of Eden came with mature trees that bore fruit, and Adam and Eve were created as adults, not babies.

It is reasonable to assume, therefore, that the universe was created as a functioning whole, and that it did not evolve from

---

[36] https://en.wikipedia.org/wiki/Solar_System.

chaos, as modern science teaches, but originated in the mind of God and was then spoken into being. "Then God said, 'Let there be light'; and there was light."

As explained in the chapter on The Importance of a Worldview, the Bible tells us that the Sun, Moon and heavens move *over the earth*, just as they are observed to do.

Modern science believes that the Sun, like other stars, evolved after the Big Bang from clouds of gas and dust that coalesced over billions of years under the force of gravity.[37] [38] The theory, of course, is contradictory to the creation account, which tells us that the Sun did not evolve over eons of time, but was created in a single day.

The Bible furthermore teaches that the stars, Sun and Moon give off their own light (e.g., Isa. 13:10) and can change their light (e.g., Joel 3:15). But astronomers believe that the stars and Sun cannot change their light and that moonlight is caused by the light of the Sun reflecting off the surface of the Moon.[39]

What the Bible says about these things is contrary to the teachings of modern science. In fact, they are anathema to it. But they are just a few of the many aspects about the world that are revealed in the Bible. Other differences have already been seen in this book, and we will see more. They make the Bible completely different from all other books, unworldly, if you will, having a wisdom of its own, a wisdom that does not come from the world.

---

[37] https://coolcosmos.ipac.caltech.edu/ask/7-How-hot-is-the-Sun.

[38] https://en.wikipedia.org/wiki/Observable_universe.

[39] For a detailed discussion of these arguments, and the truth about other aspects of modern science's understanding of the nature of the world, please refer to the book, The Flat Earth Revisited, by S. H. Shepherd.

Chapter 11 The Flood

In the six hundredth year
of Noah's life, in the
second month,

Image taken from the Web.

"In the six hundredth year of Noah's life, in the second month, the seventeenth day of the month, on that day all the fountains of the great deep were broken up, and the windows of heaven were opened." - Gen. 7:11.

The Bible tells us that a worldwide flood was God's punishment on mankind for his violent and perverse acts. The Flood reveals a lot about God and a lot about man. If God created the world, and of course He did, then He certainly has a right to destroy it when His favorite creation perverts its ways. We all need to remember this, as well as what Shakespeare said, "The evil that men do lives after them."

Unfortunately, this punishment did not change man's ways, as clearly seen throughout the Bible after the Flood, and throughout history after that time.

It was revealed to Noah, who, of all the world, was righteous in the sight of God, what God was about to do. God gave Noah the plan for building a ship, the Ark, that would save him, his wife and his three sons and their wives (eight souls altogether) from the destruction that would come upon the earth after 120 years, which, apparently, was the time that God gave mankind to repent of its iniquity. God's forbearance is reflected in these 120 years, but it is further reflected in the fact that Methuselah lived the longest of any man. His name means, "When he is dead it shall be sent." The day that Methuselah died, the flood was sent.

Noah was 600 years old when the Flood waters came upon the earth. According to the Bible, the first people on earth lived to very great ages. Adam lived to 930 years. Methuselah lived 969 years. Prior to the Flood, the average human lifespan was about 900 years. However, immediately after the Flood, when animal food was permitted to be eaten, the average lifespan fell to about 400 years. Later, when Jacob, the father of the twelve tribes of Israel, lived, the average lifespan was only about 150 years. Based on the latest worldwide statistics from WHO, the average human lifespan is currently 72 years.[40]

God instructed Noah to take with him a male and female of all animal species in order to repopulate the earth after the Flood. He also told Noah that the animals would come to him for safekeeping before the Flood would be unleashed "to destroy all flesh, wherein is the breath of life, from under heaven, and everything that is in the earth shall die." (Gen. 6:17).

Instead of what is commonly believed and taught in school, if they teach anything about the Bible in school these days, it wasn't

---

[40] The diet of our progenitors, who lived before the Flood, is described in detail in A Cristian Diet by S.H. Shepherd.

Noah who rounded up the animals, but the animals were instructed by God to go to Noah.

At the end of 120 years, which some say was how long it took Noah and his sons to build the Ark, and after all was loaded, God ordered Noah and his family to get inside. Then God shut him in, or sealed the door, and only then came the rain. It rained for 40 days and 40 nights (that is, 40 complete days), which is a long time for it to rain.

However, the fact is that many places on earth have experienced rainfalls exceeding 40 days. For example, Hawaii often experiences measurable rainfall for more than 200 days in a row.[41] The world record rainfall in any 24-hour period occurred at Foc-Foc on the French island of Réunion in the Indian Ocean in 1966, where 71.8 inches or about 6 feet fell.[42]

If we assume the world's record rainfall lasting for 40 days, not in just one place but throughout the world at the same time, which is something only God could do, it amounts to only 240 feet of water on the earth. But the Bible tells us that the mountains were covered with water: "Fifteen cubits upward did the waters prevail; and the mountains were covered." (Gen. 7:20.)

Mount. Everest, the highest peak in the world, is a little over 29,000 ft. (8839 m). Therefore, the Flood waters had to be in excess of that height. This is confirmed by climbers who have trekked to the top of Mt. Everest; they have brought back rocks containing fossils of sea lilies.[43]

---

[41] https://weather.com/news/weather/news/rain-331-da.

[42] https://www.guinnessworldrecords.com/world-records/greates.

[43] https://weather.com/en-IN/india/news/news/2018-06-29-fish-fossil-himalayas.

Obviously, it took much more than rainfall for the Flood waters to cover the mountains. The Bible tells us where the rest of the water came from: "On that day all the fountains of the great deep were broken up, and the windows of heaven were opened." (Gen. 7:11.)

Some versions of the Bible translate "windows of heaven" as "floodgates of heaven," which portrays more of a structural versus an ethereal firmament, and supports a literal interpretation of the "waters above the firmament," as described in Gen. 1:6-8.

It is apparent, therefore, that most of the water came from the floodgates of heaven and from the fountains of the great deep, although the Bible does not tell us how much each of these sources contributed.

The Bible states that when all life on earth had been destroyed by the Flood, God sent a wind to dry up the waters (Gen. 8:1). After the waters began to subside, which took months, Noah's Ark came to rest on Mt Ararat, a 16,800-foot (5170 m) mountain located on the eastern boarder of Turkey.

Seemingly, the ark of Noah was left alone on the waters with no one to guide it. It had no rudder or other means of steering. It was like many a soul who are alone in the world, who are struggling to scrape together a living, who are going through difficulties and fears without anyone's help or support. And yet, it was not alone as it tossed and heaved upon the waters. There was an unseen hand guiding it.

There appears to have been a rapid cooldown of the world after the Flood, as evidenced by the frozen woolly mammoths found in Siberia and the ice age that occurred about that time. So much water was released during the Flood that when God sent the winds that dried up the waters it cooled down the earth in a way similar to the way temperatures drop after a rain, but much more so due to the amount of water involved and the great amount of evaporation that took place. And don't forget that the energy required to change water from a liquid to a gas (vapor) is a lot of heat energy, as we know from boiling water. The energy in this case came from the winds, and from the heat removed from the earth and atmosphere during the evaporation of the Flood waters, the extensive evaporation that caused a rapid deep freezing of the earth.

It is interesting to note that seasonal cold and heat are first mentioned in the Bible after the Flood waters subsided (Gen.8:22).

The fossil evidence as well as other evidence indicates that the earth had a warmer climate in the past. Fossils of palm trees have been found in Alaska,[44] fossils of crocodiles in New Jersey, and petrified wood in the desert.[45]

We have evidence also that, no matter where people have settled in the world, they've kept records of the occurrence of a great flood. Out of 270 such records, 81%, or four out of five, agree with the Biblical record.[46]

Further evidence comes from the volcanic eruption of Mount St. Helens in 1980, and a follow up eruption that occurred two years later that caused a mud flow.

---

[44] https://www.gi.alaska.edu/alaska-science-forum/tropical-fossils-alaska.
[45] https://www.6000years.org/frame.php?page=preflood_world.
[46] https://truthwatchers.com/evidence-world-wide-flood/.

Before the Mount St. Helens events, geologists had no clear understanding of how quickly geological strata can be formed by cataclysmic events. The mud flow from Mount St. Helens' second eruption caused a canyon 1/40 the depth of the Grand Canyon to be eroded out of solid rock in a single day.[47]

Scientists say that the Grand Canyon is a gorge formed slowly over millions of years by the Colorado River which flows through it. The Mount St. Helens mud flow contradicts modern scientific theory, and supports what many independent thinking scientists now believe – that the Grand Canyon was formed by the waters of the Biblical Flood as they receded from the earth.

"This event brought many to realize that catastrophic agents can form canyons very rapidly and that streams do not cause these canyons. Rather, the streams are there because of the canyons. Furthering this theory, LANDSAT photographs of the Grand Canyon show that it passes through an elevated plateau, suggesting that the Colorado River could not have formed the canyon because rivers flow around hills, not over them. As a result, many geologists now are leaning toward the theory of catastrophic events, such as those seen at Mt. St. Helens, to explain the cause of the Grand Canyon."[48]

"The fossil-bearing sedimentary layers deposited by the Flood can be seen exposed in the walls [of the Canyon], stacked on top of one another like a huge pile of pancakes. And the view is much the same no matter where one views the Grand Canyon."[49]

---

[47] https://creationinstruction.org/sites/default/files/ftb_55_mount_st_helens.pdf.
[48] https://creationinstruction.org/sites/default/files/ftb_55_mount_st_helens .pdf.
[49] https://answersingenesis.org/the-flood/flood-cataclysm-deposit-uniform-rock-layers/.

Flat-lying, or pancake-layered, strata, many of which are extensive in area, are observed throughout the world. The strata often cover entire regions or states, such the Tapeats Sandstone strata that covers over half of the US. Most scientists believe that such layers were deposited slowly over millions and millions of years by rivers and streams. However, there is virtually no evidence of erosion between the layers as would be the case if they were carved out by rivers or streams, and the sheer size and extent of the layers indicate that they could not have been formed merely by rivers or streams. Coupled with the fact that marine fossils are discovered buried in many of these layers, the strata appear to have been deposited by a worldwide Flood.[50]

Sea shells and other marine fossils have been found on the top of mountains all over the world, including the Sierras, the Swiss Alps and the Himalayas where Mt. Everest is located, where, as noted above, climbers have found fossils of sea lilies.

The above findings are considered incontrovertible evidence that a worldwide Flood did take place, which assures us that the Bible record is reliable. But more evidence exists. For a detailed discussion of the fossils that have been found, and those that have not been found, throughout the world that chronicle the occurrence of a worldwide flood, please refer to the book, *The Flat Earth Revisited,* by S. H. Shepherd.

The Flood is only one case where scientists have affirmed the accuracy of the Bible. For more information, the reader can refer to the following links.[51] [52]

---

[50] https://earthage.org/scientific-evidence-for-a-worldwide-flood/.

[51] https://www.josh.org/.

[52] www.premierchristianity.com › Past-Issues › March-2017.

Chapter 12 The Day the Sun and Moon Stood Still, and Other Miracles

Have you not known? Have you not heard? Has it not been told you from the beginning? Have you not understood from the foundations of the earth?" - Isa. 40:21.

All expressions of Scripture are consistent with the fact that the Sun and Moon are in motion, not the earth. Never does Scripture indicate anything to the contrary. Those who read the Bible become convinced of this truth sooner or later.

The same Spirit that works in the Book of Genesis works throughout the Bible, giving in its words an unparalleled record of wisdom and integrity. The Bible is not the result of man's imagination or contriving. It is not a product of the human mind at all, any more than Nature is the product of the human mind. Its words are written "not of the will of the flesh or the will of man, but of God." (John 1:13).

David, who wrote about half of the 150 Psalms, said, "The Spirit of the Lord spoke by me, and His Word was on my tongue." - 2 Sam. 23:2.

Many people believe that the Bible is antiquated and has no application to today's world. Others believe that it cannot be taken literally because of its use of poetic language. The typical reasoning used to justify these claims includes: since no one can walk on water, then certainly Jesus could not have done so, and since no one can survive consuming fire, then Shadrach, Meshach, and Abed-Nego could not have done it.

However, as mentioned in the chapter on Hell, it is precisely because the Bible is the Word of God that it can be taken literally, and trusted implicitly. It is unlike any other book ever written. It challenges everyday thinking on every one of its pages. It was meant to be taken literally, for how else could anyone be sure of their salvation?

Our Lord, Himself, refers to the teachings of the Old Testament, including the Flood and Noah's Ark. If no worldwide Flood occurred, then surely it would be inconsistent to ask anyone to believe in Jesus Christ.

All of its teachings and precepts apply to our generation, just as they have to countless of generations before us, and, if the human race survives this century, it will apply equally well to countless of generations yet to see the light of day, for this is God's purpose.

The Bible does employ figurative, or poetic, language, including allegorical, or metaphorical, language, but it does so in a way that is similar to how we use such language in every day speech. For example, it is common practice to say such things as, "He wolfed down his food," "Lend me a hand," "I'm dead tired," or "It's raining cats and dogs."

Examples of figurative, or poetic, language used in the Bible are as follows.

"I am poured out like water, and all My bones are out of joint; My heart is like wax; it has melted within Me." - Ps. 22:14.[53]

"He raises up the poor from the dust; he lifts the needy from the

---

[53] Prophesized by David of Jesus's crucifixion ordeal.

ash heap to make them sit with princes and inherit a seat of honor. For the pillars of the earth are the Lord's, and on them He has set the world." - 1 Sam. 2:8.

"The way of the just is uprightness; O Most Upright, You weigh the path of the just." - Isa. 26:7.

"My people have committed two evils: they have forsaken me, the fountain of living waters, and hewed out cisterns for themselves, broken cisterns, that can hold no water." - Jer. 2:13.

"They trample the head of the poor into the dust of the earth." - Amos 2:7.

"I am the Vine, you are the branches. He who abides in Me, and I in him, bears much fruit." - John 15:5.

Can anyone seriously doubt that these passages of Scripture can be taken literally?

Whoever delves into Scripture sooner or later is faced with having to accept or reject its simple truths, because the Word of God gives us no other choice. It even tells us how difficult it is for people to remain faithful to its ordinances and precepts, including the laws that were given to Moses on Mt. Sinai, and the laws inscribed on the hearts of men and women in every generation by Jesus Christ.

The Day the Sun and the Moon Stood Still

"Then Joshua spoke to the Lord when the Lord delivered up the Amorites before the children of Israel, and he said in the sight of Israel:

"Sun, stand still over Gibeon;
And Moon, in the Valley of Aijalon."
So the Sun stood still,
And the Moon stopped,
Till the people had revenge
Upon their enemies.
Is this not written in the Book of Jasher?
So the Sun stood still in the midst of heaven,
And did not hasten to go down for about a whole day.
And there has been no day like that,
Before it or after it, that the Lord heeded the voice of a man;
for the Lord fought for Israel." - Josh. 10:12-14.[54]

Some say that a miracle wasn't performed at the Battle of Gibeon, but that the entire passage is an example of poetic language that cannot be taken literally. However, the Battle of Gibeon is a good example of where Scripture can be taken literally.

Why are we so quick to deny the existence of miracles, including, but not limited to, those described in the Bible? Could it be that we, like scientists, want everything to agree with our preconceptions? Miracles, by definition, are weird and hard to believe occurrences. This particular miracle is so difficult to believe that many run for cover, cover being anything that could explain it away in terms of accepted scientific theory.

Stopping the Sun and Moon in their motions over the earth was not the only miracle performed at the Battle of Gibeon. Hailstones and lightening were directed at the enemy which caused more

---

[54] Joshua commanded the Sun and Moon to stand still. He did not order the earth to stop rotating, which he could have done, because, as discussed in the chapter on the Creation, Scripture teaches that it is the Sun and Moon that moves, not the earth.

destruction than the edge of the sword. It was only after performing these miracles that God stopped the Sun and the Moon for about a whole day at Joshua's plea, thereby allowing the attack to continue until total victory was achieved.

Joshua's wars were won by God. But Israel had to fight them. God helps us in the battles of life, but we must do our part. As portrayed in the gospel story about the loaves and fishes, He blesses our actions, but only after we make the required efforts. The Lord restored Job's losses only after he had prayed for his friends. A divine law appears to be in effect, that blessings come after obedience, not before.

If you don't believe the miracles that were worked for Joshua that day, then you'll probably not believe many of the other miracles that are recorded in the Bible. For example:

When the children of Israel departed from Egypt led by Moses, God parted the Red Sea for them to escape from the Egyptian Army and then brought it down on their pursuers. Before that, God performed ten miracles in Egypt, which included turning the waters of the Nile into blood, turning the dust of the land into lice, plagues of many kinds, and three days of thick darkness that could be felt (Exodus Chapters 7-12).

Have you ever lived in a desert region of the world? Have you ever experienced its extreme dryness and gone without water for any length of time? I have lived in Arizona for quite some time, and I can tell you that the desert for most of the year is very dry; and you must drink a lot of water to make it through the day. The Egyptians, who got their water from the Nile, were deprived of it until they learned to dig holes in the ground next to the river so the sand would filter the blood out of the water. Have you ever felt darkness? I never have, but I scuba-dive and have felt the ocean all around me, and I can imagine what it is like. Scripture says that none of the Egyptians rose from their place for three days because of the thick darkness. How awful but necessary these things must have been!

During Israel's desert journeys, God brought forth rivers of water out of rock and provided manna which fed the Israelites for forty years until they crossed over the River Jordan. As mentioned in the chapter on Additional Signs of God's Displeasure, on one occasion God used a tree to work the miracle of Marah through the hand of Moses, turning water unfit for drinking into palatable water (Ex. 15:23-25). He also used a tree for crucifying His only Son.

In the New Testament, we have the stilling of the wind and the waves; the feeding of the four and the five thousand, the raising of the dead, healing of lepers, transforming water into wine, etc.

A miracle often repeated in the Bible is the raising of the dead. It occurs three times in the Old Testament and seven times in the New Testament.[55] It emphasizes the importance of the resurrection in the last days, when all souls will be summoned to appear before God.

"Your dead shall live; together with my dead body they shall arise. Awake and sing, you who dwell in dust; for your dew is like the dew of herbs, and the earth shall cast out the dead." - Isa. 26:19.

The Day the Sun Went Back on Its East to West Course

---

[55] 1 Kings 17:17-24, 2 Kings 4:32-37, 2 Kings 13:20-21, Matt. 27:50-53, Luke 7:11-15, Luke 8:41-55, John 11:1-44, Acts 9:36-41, Acts 20:9-10, and Jesus was raised form the dead as recorded in all Gospels but John, such as in Luke 24:5-6.

This miracle is recorded in the Bible four times.[56] It took place in Judea during the reign of king Hezekiah in about 715-686 BC.

King Hezekiah was struck with the sickness of which he was going to die. He was visited by Isaiah the prophet who told him that he would recover from his sickness and that God would show him a sign to prove it. He asked him to choose between two miracles, the shadow of the Sun going forward ten degrees on the sundial or going backwards ten degrees.

Hezekiah replied, "It is an easy thing for the shadow to go down ten degrees; no, but let the shadow go backward ten degrees."

For the Sun to go backward ten degrees on the sundial it would have to deviate from its normal east to west journey over the earth, and move from west to east.

Isaiah cried out to the Lord, and He brought the shadow on the sundial ten degrees backwards.

Such an occurrence would not only have been seen in Jerusalem, but throughout the daylight world. It astounded the Babylonians so much that, without having engaged in battle with Judea, they came in subjection to Hezekiah, bearing gifts and imagining him to be equal to God.

"However, regarding the ambassadors of the princes of Babylon, whom they sent to him [Hezekiah] to inquire about the wonder that was done in the land…." - 2 Chron. 32:31.

In substantiating the miracle, the Babylonians, which were perhaps the foremost of the ancient astronomers, experts at

---

[56] Isaiah 38:8, 1 Kings 20:11, 2 Kings 20:10-11 and 2 Chronicles 32:31.

observing, predicting and cataloging the movements of the heavenly bodies, testified to its authenticity.

Wikipedia states that a significant increase in the quality and frequency of Babylonian astronomical observations appeared about this time [or possibly a short time thereafter], allowing them to discover the 18-year periodicity of solar eclipses.[57]

The Day of the Three-Hour Solar Eclipse

Of all the miracles recorded in the Bible, this one ranks way up there.

According to Mark's Gospel, Jesus was crucified at the third hour of the day (9 AM) and died at the ninth hour (3 PM).[58] We also learn that from the sixth hour (noon) to the ninth hour, darkness fell over all the land.

Over the years, astronomers and historians have tried but in vain to explain the darkness that fell over Jerusalem during Jesus's crucifixion. To my knowledge, none of them has attributed the darkness to a total solar eclipse. Why? Because a total solar eclipse typically lasts about 10 minutes.[59]

So, what caused the unusual darkness? It has been conjectured that clouds or the ashes of a recently exploded volcano blanketed the area, etc. However, I firmly believe that it was none other than a very unusual total solar eclipse that lasted for about 3 solid hours, for the reasons that are given below.

---

[57] https://en.wikipedia.org/wiki/History_of_astronomy.

[58] Death from crucifixion usually took days, but Jesus's death was an exception, for He gave up His spirit at the ninth hour, as recorded in Scripture.

[59] According to the www.space.com › 15584-solar-eclipses, a total solar eclipse typically lasts 7-8 minutes.

The Gospel of Luke ascribes the three-hour period of darkness to something that obscured the Sun, "the Sun was darkened." Of the four gospel writers, Luke the physician (Col. 4:14), is the only one that had a scientific mind. Therefore, his description of the event can be expected to be the most accurate scientifically.

The crucifixion darkness has obvious significance since it is described in all four Gospels, Matthew, Mark, Luke and John. Of all the miracles recorded in the New Testament, only one other, the "Feeding of the 5,000," is mentioned in all four Gospels.

According to the Biblical account, the unusual darkness was seen not only by those who witnessed Christ's crucifixion, which included the Roman soldiers who executed Him and those who stood by watching, but by all who were in Jerusalem at the time, which was a great deal of people, consisting of thousands of devout Jews from all the surrounding nations as well as thousands of proselytes, all of whom were gathered for the great high feast of Passover that occurred once a year.

Enter now Dionysius the Areopagite, who should not be confused with "Pseudo-Dionysius the Areopagite" who lived in the fifth and sixth centuries AD, but the Dionysius who lived in Athens during the time when the Apostle Paul was in Greece in the first century AD.

It is known that the Apostle Paul visited Greece in 51 AD.[60]

Dionysius apparently was converted to Christianity after hearing Paul preach his famous sermon on Mars Hill at the Areopagus. Acts 17:34 mentions him by name, "Dionysius the Areopagite," "Areopagite" meaning a member of the Athenian conciliation court

---

[60] http://www.abrock.com/Greece-Turkey/athens.html.

of Areopagus. The same passage of Scripture says that Dionysius followed Paul after his sermon.

But before Dionysius met Paul, he was in Heliopolis, Egypt on the day when Jesus Christ was crucified. It was on that very day that he, those he was visiting, and others in that city observed an unusual solar eclipse. The eclipse they saw was unusual for several reasons. For one, an eclipse of the Sun was not due to occur at that time. For another, it lasted much longer than normal. Other irregular aspects are provided below. We know these facts because the event was recorded in Dionysius' letters to Saint Polycarp (69-155 AD), an early Church father who later died a martyr bound and burned at the stake and stabbed when the fire failed to consume his body.

The footnoted link[61] provides the letter that Dionysius wrote to Polycarp describing the event. It is in Section II of his 7th letter to Polycarp. The following excerpt is taken from that letter:

"Say to him, however, "What do you affirm concerning the eclipse, which took place at the time of the saving Cross?" For both of us at that time, at Heliopolis, being present, and standing together, saw the Moon approaching the Sun, to our surprise (for it was not the appointed time for conjunction); and again, from the ninth hour to the evening, supernaturally placed back again into a line opposite the Sun. And remind him also of something further. For he knows that we saw, to our surprise, the contact itself beginning from the east, and going towards the edge of the Sun's disc, then receding back, and again, both the contact and the re-clearing, not taking place from the same point, but from that diametrically opposite. So great are the supernatural things of that appointed

---

[61] Dionysius the Areopagite's seventh letter to Polycarp. It is available for viewing on http://www.tertullian.org/fathers/areopagite_08_letters.htm.

time, and possible to Christ alone, the Cause of All, who worketh great things and marvelous, of which there is not number."

This account explains how darkness fell over all the land in the early afternoon of Good Friday and lasted for about 3 hours. It details how the Moon was observed to eclipse the Sun, how it went back and forth over it, and credits the miracle to God as a sign of His displeasure at the death of His Son. It was when God frowned.

It reminds us once again of the awesome and incredible power God has over His created world.

"He alone spreads out the heavens and treads on the waves of the sea. He made the Bear, Orion, and the Pleiades, and the chambers of the south. He does great things past finding out, yes, wonders without number." - Job: 8-10.

Unlike man's words, the Word of God is without half-truths, exaggerations, fabrications or prideful flaunting of achievements. The lack of such things makes the Bible dull reading for those used to being entertained, but it is a veritable goldmine for seekers of the truth.

To summarize, the Bible tells us that the darkness that fell over the land at the time of the crucifixion of Christ was something that obscured the Sun, "the Sun was darkened." It is explained by a very unusual total eclipse of the Sun that was witnessed for us by Dionysius the Areopagite – the same Dionysius who is mentioned in Acts 17:34 – when he was in Heliopolis, Egypt on the day of the crucifixion. The extraordinary event tells us once again that the Bible can be taken literally.

"All your words are true." - Ps. 119:160.

"Sanctify them through thy truth; thy Word is truth." - John 17:17.

The inviolability and integrity of the Scriptures has been, and continues to be, the most time-tested and inescapable truth of all history.

It is my belief that the world is not third from the Sun, but the only world of the Son.

Chapter 13 Who is God, the Great King?

The Scriptures reveal many attributes of God's nature, including His human qualities as given in John's gospel and Hebrews. But they do not end there, for many passages portray Him as a great king, bristling in righteousness, strong in power, but also compassionate and understanding. His supreme sovereignty over man is treated throughout this book, but this chapter will focus on His other characteristics, those that describe Him more fully, for it is in them that He is personally revealed.

Before we begin, however, let us ask ourselves a simple question. Who is God, really?

Basically, He is completeness, the all, the totality. He created everything of a non-material nature and all that can be seen, heard and felt. Moreover, it is in Him that all things consist. We pass away, but He lives forever. Nothing existed before Him, and He is the only god there is. Everything is done by His consent, with His foreknowledge and for His purposes, no matter how mysterious or incomprehensible it may seem to us. It is the way things are, for so He has prepared it.

The Bible is the self-revelation of God. From Genesis to Revelation, God reveals Himself as invisible, eternal, holy, omnipotent, omnipresent and omniscient (for example, Job 34:21, Prov. 15:3, and Ps. 139:3). We know that He is spirit (John 4:24).

He is the Father of lights.

"Every good gift and every perfect gift is from above, and comes down from the Father of lights, with whom there is no variation or shadow of turning." - James 1:17 (NSAB and NKJV).

He is light, and in Him there is no darkness at all (1 John 1:5, Heb. 1:3).

He is blinding light; He dwells in unapproachable light (1 Tim. 6:16). No one has ever seen Him or can see Him (Ex. 33:20, John 1:18, 1 Tim. 6:16).

His light shines in the darkness and the darkness cannot overcome it (John 1:5). It was on the road to Damascus that Paul, blinded by the Divine light, heard Jesus speak. The Apostle's course was then set, his marching orders given to him. He evangelized with this light the Roman world, and his elucidating and enlightening epistles are the result.

Moses was able to talk with Him, but not see Him, sometimes for long periods of time, and when he appeared back in the camp, the skin of his face shone, and it shone bright enough to frighten the people so that they demanded he wear a veil over his face whenever he talked with them (Ex. 34:29-35).

Who can stand before a holy God? It is why He has given all authority on heaven and earth, including judgment authority, to Jesus, and it is in the presence of Jesus that all of us must someday appear.

God has emotions. For example, He loves and hates. Malachi 1::2-3 declares: "'I have loved you,'" says the Lord. But you ask, 'How have you loved us?' 'Was not Esau Jacob's brother?', the Lord says. 'Yet I have loved Jacob, but Esau I have hated, and I have turned his mountains into a wasteland and left his inheritance to the desert jackals."

"You hate all workers of iniquity. You shall destroy those who speak falsehood; the Lord abhors the bloodthirsty and deceitful man." - Ps. 5:5-6.

"The fear of the Lord is to hate evil; pride and arrogance, and the evil way and the perverse mouth I hate." - Prov. 8:13.

"These six things the Lord hates, yes, seven are an abomination to Him: A proud look, a lying tongue, hands that shed innocent blood, a heart that devises wicked plans, feet that are swift in running to evil, a false witness who speaks lies, and one who sows discord among brethren." - Prov. 6:16-19.

"Do not plot evil against each other, and do not love to swear falsely. I hate all this, declares the Lord." - Zech. 8:17.

"Those who honor Me I will honor." – 1 Sam. 2:30.

His compassion is revealed throughout the Bible (e. g., Ps. 34:18, 2 Cor. 1:3-4, Rom. 8:26 and 8:28, 1 Pet. 5:10). At Lazarus' tomb, He wept.[62]

In Genesis 6:6, God expresses grief:

"And the Lord was sorry that He had made man on the earth, and He was grieved in His heart."

Then there is jealousy. Like all great kings of the earth, God demands loyalty. He is a jealous God.

"Thou shalt not make unto thee any graven image, or any likeness." (Ex. 20:4). In these words, God forbids us to make,

---

[62] Alexander Maclaren said that the tears of Christ are the pity of God.

and, if you extrapolate the thought, to think about Him as the likeness of anything on earth.

"You shall not bow down to them nor serve them. For I, the Lord your God, am a jealous God, visiting the iniquity of the fathers upon the children to the third and fourth generations of those who hate Me." - Ex. 20:5.

Also, there is joy:

"Yes, I will rejoice over them to do them good, and I will assuredly plant them in this land, with all My heart and with all My soul." - Jeremiah 32:41.

God is perfect in all ways. No mortal can attain to perfection, but He is perfection personified. His power, righteousness, justice, goodness, forbearance, love, mercy and compassion are boundless, as He is boundless. No hyperbole can adequately describe Him.

He is total Being, always present; always seeing and always knowledgeable of everything that goes on.

"Great is our Lord, and mighty in power, His understanding is infinite." - Ps. 147:5.

"I AM WHO I AM." - Ex. 3:14.

"Before Abraham was, I AM." - John 48:58.

He is the Ancient of Days.

"I watched till thrones were put in place, and the Ancient of Days was seated. His garment was white as snow, and the hair of His head was like pure wool. His throne was a fiery flame, its wheels a burning fire. A fiery stream issued and came forth from before Him. A thousand thousands ministered to Him. Ten thousand times ten thousand stood before Him. The court was seated, and the books were opened." - Dan. 7:9-10.

Paul says in Colossians, and also in Hebrews, that Jesus is the image of God, and that through Him all things were created.

"He is the image of the invisible God, the firstborn over all creation. For by Him all things were created that are in heaven and that are on earth, visible and invisible, whether thrones or dominions or principalities or powers. All things were created through Him and for Him. And He is before all things, and in Him all things consist." - Col. 1:15-17.

Jesus gave us our most complete picture of the Father. As John states in his gospel, "The only begotten Son, who is in the bosom of the Father, He has declared Him." By the teachings and example of Christ, we have, perhaps, our clearest understanding of God, Himself.

John's knowledge of Jesus was more intimate than many others who knew Him, for John had known Jesus from the start of His ministry, when he was a disciple of John the Baptist, as did Andrew, his brother Peter, and also Nathaniel.

Philip, summing up the seeming quandary that the disciples had about who Jesus was, stated the following:

"Philip said to Him, 'Lord, show us the Father, and it is sufficient for us.' Jesus said to him, 'Have I been with you so long, and yet you have not known Me, Philip? He who has seen Me has seen the Father; so how can you say, 'Show us the Father'? Do you not believe that I am in the Father, and the Father in Me? The words that I speak to you I do not speak on My own authority; but the Father who dwells in Me does the works." - John 14:8-9.

As Matthew Henry puts it this way in his commentary:

"All that saw Christ by faith, saw the Father in Him. In the light of Christ's doctrine, they saw God as the Father of lights; and in Christ's miracles, they saw God as the God of power. The holiness of God shone in the spotless purity of Christ's life."[63]

God is portrayed as having masculine traits, and nowhere in Scripture is He portrayed otherwise.

Glory and honor are His clothing. He chooses to dwell in thick darkness to protect us. In Exodus 33:20, God told Moses that no man could see Him and live. When the tabernacle was completed the glory of God was manifested in a dense cloud that covered it and prevented Moses from entering it (Ex. 40:34).

"Clouds and thick darkness are all around Him." - Ps. 97:2.

When Solomon finished his temple of gold in Jerusalem, a cloud filled it and the priests could not perform their service because of the cloud, for the glory of the Lord filled the temple. Then Solomon said, 'The Lord has said that he would dwell in a dark cloud; I have indeed built a magnificent temple for you, a place for you to dwell forever.'" (1 Kings 8:10-13). Then he said, "But will God indeed dwell on the earth? Behold, heaven and the heaven of heavens cannot contain You. How much less this temple which I have built!" (1 Kings 8:27).

---

[63] Matthew Henry's Concise Commentary, John 14:1-11.

But no matter how much we know about God, there will always be a dark cloud of unknowing between us. We must come to grips with the reality that although we know a lot about God from the Bible, He is basically an unknown quantity. We cannot explain Him, at least not completely. How can a Being exist that "has no beginning and no end?

"You are My witnesses," says the Lord, and My servant whom I have chosen, that you may know and believe Me, and understand that I am He. Before Me there was no God formed, nor shall there be after Me." - Isa. 43:10.

We cannot fully comprehend the glory and magnitude of God, even with the Holy Spirit, because we have finite minds and God is infinite and eternal, and we only receive a portion of the Spirit when we come to accept Jesus as the truth (Acts 2:38). The things He wants us to know about Him, these are the things that we know. But there is much mystery about Him, and no one has ever been able to completely explain God.

"Can you search out the deep things of God? Can you find out the limits of the Almighty? They are higher than heaven – what can you do? Deeper than Sheol – what can you know?" - Job 11:7-8.

"No one can fathom what God has done from beginning to end." - Eccl. 3:11.

It is written in the Book of Isaiah:

"For My thoughts are not your thoughts, nor are your ways My ways," says the Lord. For as the heavens are higher than the earth, so are My ways higher than your ways, and My thoughts than your thoughts." - Isa. 55:8-9.

If we believe that God's omniscience far surpasses man's abilities to comprehend, and do not underestimate or put limits on His omnipotence, then we are beginning to fear Him.

"The fear of the Lord is the beginning of wisdom, and the knowledge of the Holy One is understanding." - Prov. 9:10.

God said of Job that, at the time he lived, there was none like him on the earth who feared God and shunned evil (Job 2:3).

God wants us to fear Him, and much of what He does is done for that purpose (Eccl. 3:14).

We were created in His image, so He is a person somewhat like ourselves, but He is so much more than His creation. He speaks into existence the earth, Moon, Sun, stars, planets and the other celestial bodies, and life on earth. He is the bright morning star, the firstborn of all creation, and the fountain of living waters. He is the everlasting God (Gen. 21:33), the Sustainer of Life, and the Prize of Salvation. He is the Possessor of Heaven and earth (Gen. 14:22). He is high and lifted up. His thoughts are not our thoughts, nor are our ways His ways.

There is no superlative of merit that cannot be ascribed to Him. He is a consuming fire (Deut. 4:24, Isa.66:15-16 and Heb. 12:29). He formed man from the dust of the ground and breathed into his nostrils the breath of life, and man became a living being (Gen. 2:7). No one else can do these things. We are similar to God in certain ways, having a soul, or spirit, given to us at birth along with emotions, feelings, creativity, and the fact that each of us is unique; but that's about it, for none of us are immortal or eternal, nor are we omniscient, omnipresent or omnipotent.

It is important to understand what would happen if a person were to see God in His full glory. In short, it would be instant death (Ex. 33:20), for man is not capable of taking the blinding light and living through the experience. Ever had your breath taken away by something that was truly spectacular? Multiply it by a million or a billion and you get the idea. While God is within the reaches of our intellect, we can never see Him as He really is. It is fair to say that He dwells in a dark cloud of mystery; He is beyond our ability to fully comprehend.

"To whom will you liken Me, and make Me equal and compare Me, that we should be alike?" - Isa. 46:5.

"I am God, and there is no other; I am God, and there is none like Me, declaring the end from the beginning, and from ancient times things that are not yet done." - Isa. 46:9-10.

Charles H. Spurgeon, the great English preacher and theologian of the 19th century, said that no one can explain how the Spirit of God breathes into the soul the breath of life.

He can read our minds; He knows our thoughts ("For I *know* their works and their thoughts." - Isa. 66:18).. It was clearly revealed during Jesus' ministry on earth. Jesus knew what people were thinking. He knew their intentions and their motives. He understood them perfectly, as He does us. An example is given after the miraculous feeding of the 4,000, when the people who had seen his disciples enter into a boat without Him searched all night and came to the other side where the boat had landed, and there was Jesus.

"Rabbi, how comest thou here?", asked the people. Instead of answering the question, Jesus replied, "Truly, truly, I say unto you, you seek Me not because you saw signs, but because you ate of the loaves." (John 6:25-26.) He knew they wanted to make Him king so that they could eat plentifully thereafter.

Other passages that reveal Jesu's ability to read minds include that of the rich young ruler who asked Jesus how he may have eternal life (Matt. 19:16-25), and when a man approached Him as He was journeying on the road and said to Him that he would follow Him wherever He went (Luke 9:57-58), Jesus said to him, knowing his thoughts, that foxes have holes and birds have nests, but the Son of man has nowhere to lay His head. We do not know whether the man followed Him or not, but we assume that he did since nothing otherwise is recorded about the incident.

The phrase, "come to know God" is an expression commonly used by the church. However, we can never really know Him (1 John 3:2) until heaven reveals Him to us.

Luke's parable of the *Ten Minas* (Luke 19:11-27) testifies that God is a great King, one who is fair to those He favors by giving them rewards for their stewardship, but who executes severe punishment on His enemies.

"Then he said to those standing by, 'Take his mina away from him and give it to the one who has ten minas.'" 'Sir,' they said, 'he already has ten!' "He replied, 'I tell you that to everyone who has, more will be given, but as for the one who has nothing, even what they have will be taken away. But those enemies of mine who did not want me to be king over the — bring them here and kill them in front of me.'" - Luke 19:24-27.

The Book of Malachi tells us:

"'For I am a great King,' says the Lord of hosts. and My name is to be feared among the nations. Your eyes shall see, and you shall say, 'The Lord is magnified beyond the border of Israel." - Mal. 1:4-6.

It is written in the Book of Romans:

"As I live, says the Lord, every knee shall bow to Me, and every tongue shall confess to God." - Rom. 14:11.

Similarly, Isaiah:

"I have sworn by Myself; the word has gone out of My mouth in righteousness, and shall not return, that to Me every knee shall bow, every tongue shall take an oath." - Is. 45:33.

"Heaven is my throne, and the earth is my footstool." - Is. 66:1 and Acts 7:49.

"Great is our Lord, and mighty in power, His understanding is infinite." - Ps. 147:5.

Scripture passages such as these, and the arresting message of the winnowing fan, do what other passages cannot do — they give us a profound respect and veneration for the Creator. They make us realize that the Lord is not to be trifled with. He knows all things and sees all things. Nothing is hidden from His eyes. God is a loving God, but He is also our righteous and Sovereign King. If we think often on these things, they instill in us a right view of Him.

"Ascribe to the Lord the glory due His name; worship the Lord in the splendor of His holiness. The voice of the Lord is over the waters; the God of glory thunders, the Lord thunders over the mighty waters. The voice of the Lord is powerful; the voice of the Lord is majestic." - Ps. 29:1-4.

"He who is the blessed and only Potentate, the King of kings and Lord of lords, who alone has immortality, dwelling in unapproachable light, whom no man has seen or can see, to whom be honor and everlasting power. Amen." - 1 Tim. 6:15-16.

God is the epitome of every virtue that we can attribute to a great king, so much so that He is difficult to fully comprehend.

We know that whatever He does, it is forever. Nothing can be added to it, and nothing taken from it, that men should fear Him (Eccl. 3:14).

All of these Scriptures taken together make Him the great unfathomable Being. We can know about Him, but we do not know exactly what He is. Many have tried to penetrate the mystery of God, including St. John of the Cross; the author of the medieval treatise, *The Cloud of Unknowing*, and Julian of Norwich, but none have come up with a more precise answer.

"The higher part of contemplation, insofar as it is possible to possess it here below, consists mainly in this cloud of unknowing, with a loving impulse and a dark gazing into the simple being of God Himself alone... for as long as the soul dwells in this mortal body, the clarity of our understanding in the contemplation of all spiritual things, and especially of God, is always mixed up with some sort of imaginations." - Author (anonymous) of *The Cloud of Unknowing.*

It is written in the Book of Deuteronomy:

"The secret things belong to the Lord our God, but those things which are revealed belong to us and to our children forever." - Deut. 29:29.

Chapter 14 Heaven — What Is It Like?

"Set your minds on things above, not on things that are on earth."
- Col. 3:2.

The Bible gives us few details about heaven, but what it provides is sufficient to allow us to understand what may be expected, and some of the particulars are very interesting.

First, the afterlife in general. The Bible indicates in the Old Testament that when physical death occurs the soul (or spirit) first goes to a place of rest and stays in restful darkness until the Day of Judgment (Job 3:5, Job 10:22, Job 17:16). 1 Kings 2:10 (NKJV) states, "So David rested with his fathers." The KJV is more specific in that it uses "slept" instead of "rested." Jesus said that the little girl was not dead but sleeping, and Paul uses "sleep" in 1 Cor. 15:51. Apparently, the dead are (at least in God's sight) unconscious like when asleep.

Jesus's words to the repentant thief on the cross indicate that at death souls may immediately ascend to heaven (Paradise) (Luke 23:43). This is different than the Old Testament teaching. However, since time is a temporal thing, and to God one day is as a thousand years and a thousand years are as one day (2 Pet. 3:8, Ps. 90:4), I believe we may dismiss it as not being significant. In other words, it doesn't really matter.

Purgatory, which is perhaps a figment of pagan writers, is not mentioned in the Bible.

The Bible indicates that there are three heavens, the sky, outer space and heaven (often capitalized), which is God's abode,[64] and that they were created. Some believe it means that after the second coming of Christ and His millennium reign, they will be substituted by the new heavens and new earth (Isa. 65:17, Isa. 66:22, 2 Pet. 3:13, Rev. 21:1), and this is substantially consistent with the "restoration of all things" (Acts 3:21). However, the chronology of events, especially as described in the Book of Revelation, are believed by some theologians and epistemologists to be unimportant. In any case, the Holy City, the New Jerusalem, will be heaven's centerpiece (Rev. 21:2). It is called the Paradise of God. It is where righteousness dwells. God will dwell there forever with the redeemed of mankind.

Before all that occurs, however, heaven is God's throne; it is where God and the holy angels reside.

Formerly, heaven was where Satan and his fallen angels resided, for Jesus told his disciples, "I saw Satan fall from heaven like lightening." (Luke 10:18). The Book of Revelation tells us that when God expelled Satan, the great dragon, from heaven, his tail drew a third of heaven with him (Rev. 12:3-4). It is believed that one of the things they brought with them was sorcery.[65]

It is speculative because of the lack of detail in the Bible, but heaven may now exist as it always has, although its complement of souls is incomplete. As Jesus revealed in the parable of the *Wedding Feast*, and also in Scripture passages that tell us that God wants no one to perish but wishes for all to be saved, it is evident that God wants a full house.

---

[64] https://www.gotquestions.org/levels-heaven.html.

[65] According to the apocalyptic text known as the Book of Enoch (Ref. https://en.wikipedia.org. > wiki > fallen_angel).

Heaven is a place of sanctification and purity. One must be cleansed of their sins to enter its gates. No outsiders, those who are destitute of righteousness and holiness, are allowed. Do not take sin lightly, for the sinner, the sexually immoral, the idolater, the adulterer, the homosexual, the sodomite, the thief, the covetous, the drunkard, the reviler and the extortioner will not inherit the kingdom of God (1 Cor. 6:9-11). Only the repentant are allowed. Repentance is a change of heart and mind about sin; it includes turning away from sin and turning to God for forgiveness. The good thing is that the Spirit of God helps us in these matters by encouraging us to repent (Rom. 8:26).

In heaven are the Tree of Life (Rev. 2:7), and the Book of Life (for example, Ps. 69:28) in which are recorded the names of those who are counted worthy to be in heaven. It is where the Great White Throne is located (Rev. 20:11). It is called Paradise (Luke 23:43; 2 Cor. 12:1-4). It is where Jesus is, who has sat down at the right hand of God (for example, Matt. 26:64).

However, the Holy Scriptures do not reveal how heaven is configured, nor does it include many of its other details. It has been one of the great questions and mysteries of all time because no one really knows what it looks like. The Bible also does not answer all of questions we have about life after death. Billy Graham said the reason for it is because our minds are limited and heaven is far too glorious to be understood by us. But it could also be because God prefers to keep it that way – a mystery – perhaps for the testing of our faith.

"In all the things that so great and wise a God has created, there must be many secrets." - St. Teresa of Avila.

Of course, there are various concepts of heaven in the world, such as Valhalla and Nirvana. Valhalla is the name of a mythological Norse majestic hall ruled over by the god Odin, where all of the human heroic dead come together and practice for a great battle of fighting one another for eternity.[66] [67] Nirvana refers to Moksha, which is freedom from the cycle of death and rebirth.[68] But neither of them are the same thing as the heaven described in the Bible.

Notwithstanding the lack of detail concerning heaven, the Bible does tell us some interesting things about this glorious place. The word "heaven" is found numerous times in the New Testament alone.[69] Some of the passages are cited herein.

Heaven's Location

The location of heaven is not revealed in Scripture other than it is where God lives, and, with respect to the earth, it is located up, not down. We know this not only because Jesus looked up to heaven whenever he broke bread, and when He divided the loaves and fishes among the 5,000 and 4,000, but by the two men in white apparel who appeared to the disciples on the Mt. of Olives when Jesus was taken up from them, who said that was what happened to Him (Acts 1:11).[70] We also know it by the passage that describes Elijah being taken up by a whirlwind into heaven (2 Kings 2:11).

The Bible teaches that there is a firmament, a structure or a

---

[66] https://en.wikipedia.org/wiki/Nirvana.

[67] Many in the German Wehrmacht and Waffen SS believed they would attain Valhalla by valiantly defending their country.

[68] https://en.wikipedia.org/wiki/Nirvana.

[69] According to the Web, heaven is mentioned 276 times in the New Testament.

[70] According to John Gill's Exposition of the Bible, the two men were two angels in the form of men; it being usual with them to appear in human form, and that the men suddenly appeared and stood by them.

combination of ethereal and material construction, that exists over the earth, and that there is nothing outside or above it except the upper waters and heaven, which is God's abode, and that all of the world or universe as we know it is contained beneath the firmament, everything we can know and see, including the Sun, Moon, planets, stars and heavenly objects.

Merriam Webster defines "firmament" as "the vault or arch of the sky." The Book of Genesis states:

"And God said, "Let there be a vault between the waters to separate water from water." So God made the vault and separated the water under the vault from the water above it. And it was so. God called the vault "sky." And there was evening, and there was morning – the second day." - Gen. 1:6-8 (NIV).

Isaiah tells us:

Heaven is not far away. Angels are not far away. It's only that we cannot detect them with our five senses.

"We are standing on holy ground,
And I know that there are angels
All around.
Let us praise Jesus now;
We are standing on Holy ground."[71]

Angels are living creatures. They are called cherubim (plural of cherub) and seraphim, angelic beings that serve and worship God. Remember that it was cherubim whom God placed at the entrance of the Garden of Eden, together with a flaming sword, to keep man out after the Fall (Gen. 3:23-24).

---

[71] On Holy Ground was written by Geron Davis in 1960 when he was 19.

Perhaps the most important and intriguing question about heaven is, what will we be like there?

It is written in the Book of Job:

"After my skin is destroyed, this I know, that in my flesh I shall see God, whom I shall see for myself, and my eyes shall behold, and not another. How my heart yearns within me!" - Job 19:26-27.

The verse indicates many things. It indicates that we will have a body (flesh) of some kind. It cannot be human body because 1 Cor. 15:49-52 states that flesh and blood cannot inherit the kingdom of God; it appears that the word flesh here is somewhat of a figure of speech in which a word or phrase is applied to an something which it is not literally applicable. It indicates also that we will see God, and it indicates that we will see Him and not another, or that we alone will see Him, perhaps meaning that each of us who make it to heaven will see Him in some unique way. "I shall see for myself" indicates that we will no longer need a Mediator or Advocate to "see" Him, or it could mean that we will see him with our own eyes, which implies that we will have the sense of vision in heaven, which would be a wonderful thing, and which will probably be true as we will soon see, or it could mean both, as I think it does. The verse further indicates how wonderous the experience will be, "How my heart yearns within me!"

The Scriptures tell us that we will see God and Jesus in heaven (Job 19:26-27, Acts 7:55, Matt. 5:18, John 14:2-3, Rev. 22:3-4), although it may be their glory that will be seen.

The Bible teaches that no one without the Holy Spirit dwelling in them can envision with any accuracy what heaven is like. As mentioned in the chapter on the Spirit of God, God gives to all believers a measure of the Spirit. It is what allows them to penetrate vaguely, but insightfully, into the unseen world.

The Bible further teaches that heaven will be a place that is so marvelous it is above our finite minds to describe.

"Eye has not seen, nor ear heard, nor have entered into the heart of man the things which God has prepared for those who love Him. But God has revealed them to us through His Spirit. For the Spirit searches all things, yes, the deep things of God." - 1 Cor. 2:9.

John tells us in his first epistle:

"Beloved, now we are children of God; and it has not yet been revealed what we shall be, but we know that when He is revealed, we shall be like Him, for we shall see Him as He is." - 1 John 3:2-3.

Life without end! It's hard not to think about what it would be like. But we can never imagine what it is fully like, nor can we imagine what eternal punishment is fully like, although we can piece together some of it by turning to Scripture.

Jesus instructed the Pharisees, as recorded in Matthew 22:30, that in the resurrection they neither marry nor are given in marriage, but are like angels of God in heaven. Those who are considered worthy to be in heaven will not marry or think about marriage; such urges will be no longer be in us, but will be completely foreign to us, and more importantly, they will no longer burden or distract us from our work.

Paul tells us in Phil. 3:20-21:

"The Lord Jesus Christ will transform our lowly body that it may be conformed to His glorious body, according to the working by which He is able even to subdue all things to Himself."

The three verses (1 Cor. 15:49-52, 1 John 3:2-3 and Phil. 3:20-21) are about all we have to go on regarding what type of body souls assume that are counted worthy to be given eternal life in God's abode.

People know us after we die. We do not lose our identity. This is indicated in the parable of the *Rich Man and Lazarus*, an excerpt of which is:

"… The rich man also died and was buried. And being in torments in Hades, he lifted up his eyes and saw Abraham afar off, and Lazarus in his bosom. Then he cried and said, 'Father Abraham, have mercy on me, and send Lazarus that he may dip the tip of his finger in water and cool my tongue; for I am tormented in this flame.'… But Abraham said,…'And besides all this, between us and you there is a great gulf fixed, so that those who want to pass from here to you cannot, nor can those from there pass to us.'" - Luke 16:19-26.

We learn from the parable that there is little doubt that a spiritual body sees, hears and communicates.

God, Himself, who is Spirit (John 4:24), is able to communicate verbally with human beings. He spoke to Adam and Eve in the Garden of Eden. He spoke to Moses many times on the top of Mt. Saini and from the cherubim above the Ark of the covenant. He spoke to many of the prophets, some even by name, such as Amos. He announced audibly to those near Jesus that He was His only Beloved Son (Mark 1:11, Matt. 17:5-6, 2 Pet. 1:17).

"God, who at various times and in various ways spoke in time past to the fathers by the prophets, has in these last days spoken to us by His Son, whom He has appointed heir of all things, through whom also He made the worlds." - Heb. 1:1-2.

"Out of heaven He let you hear His voice, that He might instruct you; on earth He showed you His great fire, and you heard His words out of the midst of the fire." - Deut. 4:36.

He speaks to us in His Word. He speaks to us in times of trial and distress. And He wants us to speak to Him. He comforts us in every aspect of our lives.

It is likely, therefore, that souls worthy to ascend after the Judgment will see, hear and communicate in heaven. And why shouldn't they? How else would they be able to judge and rule, for in Matt. 12:25-27 and Luke 22:30 Jesus tells us that His disciples will be judges, and other passages of the Bible teach us that in the Messianic kingdom believers will rule with Christ (1 Cor. 6:2, 2 Tim. 2:12, Rev. 2:26, Rev. 20:4). A spiritual body with senses would be a wonderous thing!

I venture to say that ascenders to heaven will have aerial bodies, able to fly as well as walk. The cherubim and seraphim have wings and are able to fly (Ezek. 25:20, Isa. 6:6). It is written that those who are in the rapture will be caught up together in the clouds with those who ascend from the dead to meet the Lord in the air, and so shall we ever be with the Lord (1 Thess. 4:16-17).

The ability to fly will open a new dimension of freedom to explore an exciting, wonderous place where everywhere one looks will be endless wonders and vistas, new sights and new sensations. It will be unlike anything on earth. It will be a release instead of a narrowing.

"Oh, how great is Your goodness, which You have laid up for those who fear You, which You have prepared for those who trust in You in the presence of the sons of men!" - Ps. 31:19.

The habitation of God, theologically and eschatologically, is actually in His Son, Jesus Christ, whose purpose for the world was, and is, that men should become the dwelling place of God (for example, John 17:22-23, Rom. 8:10 and 2 Cor. 4:7) so that they can glorify Him and have communion with Him, as described previously. He came to the earth to save mankind from their sins and transform them into sons of God. That is the purpose and work of our Lord and Savior. It is accomplished through God's work of division and by the work of the Holy Spirit.

The consummation of the goal is expressed in the Bible where it says that when all things are subjected to Him, then the Son Himself also will be subjected to the One who subjected all things to Him, that God may be all in all (1 Cor. 15:28).

"For whom He foreknew, He also predestined to be conformed to the image of His Son, that He might be the firstborn among many brethren. Moreover, whom He predestined, these He also called; whom He called, these He also justified; and whom He justified, these He also glorified." - Rom. 8:29-30.

Important Characteristics of Heaven

John's revelation of the heavenly city, the New Jerusalem that comes down from heaven, is believed to be what heaven is like. It seems to be, however, an example of where the Bible may be taken figuratively, for God is capable of doing so much more than limiting the bounds of heaven to some 1500 by 1500 by 1500 miles dimensions in width, length and depth.[72]

Many believe that the "mansions" spoken of by Jesus in John 14:1-2 are literal, huge buildings or giant homes where God has prepared a place for His saints. The term "mansions" is an obvious metaphor for something that is truly stupendous, but a believer's mansion in heaven is no doubt unlike any mansion on earth, or anything that can possibly be imagined.

Like all the other attributes of God, His creativity must be boundless. The universe of the night sky appears to be boundless, and His abode no doubt extends without limit in all directions. To my way of thinking, heaven is likely to have a lot of scope, range and room, and be representative of the abode of a king of a vast domain.

Only by degrees will a sense of the strangeness of the place become evident to the new comer, and afterwards a profoundness will slowly creep in that will be the dominant feeling.

A chief characteristic of the New Jerusalem that comes down from heaven is the glory of God, the presence of God who resides in it. Revelation 22:5 and 21:1-4 reveal that heaven has no night, but that the Lord Himself is the light, and that the Sun and the Moon are no longer needed. The new Jerusalem, adorned like the bride of Christ, which may be taken as symbolic of the church of Christ, will descend from heaven like a huge, precious jewel and situate itself on the top of a great and high mountain. It will be constructed of pure gold, precious stones and pearls (Rev. 21:11-13).

---

[72] Dimensions are taken from https://en.wikipedia.org/wiki/New_Jerusalem.

There will be no more sea, or ocean, in heaven (Rev. 21:1). "Behold, I make all things new." - Rev. 21:15.

From what we can piece together from Scripture, heaven is, or will be, a place of peace, a perfect resting in God. It will be devoid of pain and all other earthly torments, including fear, anxiety, heartbreak, confusion, disillusionment and frustration. In short, it will be a place without any of the ills and misfortunes that constitute so much of life on earth.

"And God will wipe away every tear from their eyes; there shall be no more death, nor sorrow, nor crying. There shall be no more pain, for the former things have passed away." - Rev. 21:4.

"You will forget your misery; it will be like water flowing away. Your life will be brighter than the noonday. Even darkness will be as bright as morning. Having hope will give you courage. You will be protected and will rest in safety. You will lie down unafraid, and many will look to you for help." - Job 11:16-19.

Time

Perhaps the most striking characteristic of heaven will be the absence of time, which we implicitly understand from "for the old order of things has passed away" (Rev. 21:3-4), and the fact that heaven is our eternal inheritance (1 Pet. 1:3-5). No clocks will be there, for time there does not exist. Those in heaven are no longer prisoners of time, slaves of time, rushing to and fro trying to get things done on schedule, trapped in the endless maze of time. I envision them instead to be like children at play, moving from one thing to another always entranced by what they do. The new sense of freedom may be the hardest thing to get used to about the place. But it doesn't mean that there will not be work to be done there, for God will see to that.

Heaven will likely provide plenty of responsibilities, as we understand from such verses as Matt. 12:27, Matt. 25:14-30 and Luke 19:24-27, which means plenty of work to do, and all of it will be for eternity, with maybe options of branching out into new directions as needed or wished, and all of it will be a joy (Rom. 14:17).

In short, souls that make it to heaven, who satisfy its entrance requirements, will live an unburdened, unconstrained life in which the world's many constraints and artificialities are absent. It will be a realm where everything is done according to God's will. There will no longer be a wrestling or struggling with some internal or external fear, difficulty, worry or problem.

I envision heaven to be a wonderous place beautiful in elevation (Ps. 48:2), resplendent in dazzling colors and full of beauty that pleases the aesthetic senses, especially the sight, that offers its occupants a chance for endless creativity. It is not certain from Scripture, but it could be that whatever skill or craft a person had on earth will be put to good use there.

It will be a life most blessed, in which there will be no more death or suffering. It will be a place where the worthy are rewarded for their conduct on earth because these things are what constitute their treasure in heaven (e.g., Matt. 6:20-21). When Jesus is our treasure on earth, then we build on that treasure whenever we commit our resources to do His work in the world.

Other aspects about eternal life in the land of rest and peace are revealed to us in the parable of the *Talents* and the parable of the *Wise and Foolish Virgins*, both of which are discussed in a subsequent chapter. Other parables also tell us what heaven is like:

The Parable of the Hidden Treasure

"Again, the kingdom of heaven is like treasure hidden in a field, which a man found and hid; and for joy over it he goes and sells all that he has and buys that field." - Matt. 13:44.

The Parable of the Pearl of Great Price

"Again, the kingdom of heaven is like a merchant seeking beautiful pearls, who, when he had found one pearl of great price, went and sold all that he had and bought it." - Matt. 13:45-46.

These two parables compare heaven with treasure. Although they may be confusing, they indicate the extreme value of heaven.

The Parable of the Dragnet

"Again, the kingdom of heaven is like a dragnet that was cast into the sea and gathered some of every kind, which, when it was full, they drew to shore; and they sat down and gathered the good into vessels, but threw the bad away. So it will be at the end of the age. The angels will come forth, separate the wicked from among the just, and cast them into the furnace of fire. There will be wailing and gnashing of teeth." - Matt. 13:47-50.

The parable is much like that of the *Wheat and the Tares*, but instead of plants we have fishes. It echoes the message of the winnowing fan. Those whom He purposes to dwell with Him in heaven are brought ashore, and those who are not are thrown away.

The few details we have about heaven from Scripture give us enough to increase our faith and try our imagination, for we will have a new body and a new life in the glorious presence of God.

And, just as wonderous, Jesus told us that in heaven we will know everything that we do not now know. "In that day, you will ask Me nothing." (John 16:23). In that day we will feast with God and partake of His rich delights and goodness (Isa 25:6).

David said:

"As for me, I will see Your face in righteousness; I shall be satisfied when I awake in Your likeness." - Ps. 17:15.

Meanwhile, we must not forget that we have a job to do here on earth, a race to run, and to effectively do it we must stay in contact with the One who gave us new life. Let not God say of any of us,

"I have this against you, that you have left your first love." - Rev. 2:4.

Rather, let Him say:

"I know your works, your labor, your patience, and that you cannot bear those who are evil. And you have tested those who say they are apostles and are not, and have found them liars; and you have persevered and have patience, and have labored for My name's sake and have not become weary." - Rev. 2:2-3.

Chapter 15 Great Mysteries of Life

As mysterious as it may sound, we live in a world that in many ways defies understanding. It is a world not of our own making, but one in which we one day found ourselves a part.

The entire creation account is supernatural. How can anything be spoken into existence when nothing existed before? Our own existence is nothing but a miracle. Have you ever thought about it? Our introduction into this world is shrouded in mystery, as is our introduction into the spiritual world.

Modern science tells us that there is nothing that happens that cannot be explained. However, those who deny the supernatural have a hard task ahead of them to explain many things about life and this world.

That cut on the finger, how miraculously it heals itself. Or the way the body knows only by taste or smell what digestive juices to use for foods. Would these things be easy to program a computer to do?

A tree is a miracle any way you look at it. It can draw water up out of the rocks and soil through its root system and deliver it to every part of the tree, and often to very great heights, something that man cannot do without machines.

Or take the parable of the mustard seed. The tiny seed contains the potential not only for growing into a large plant but for producing many more plants. A seed is infinity in living form.

The human being is distinguished from other animals by its language capacity and ability to talk. But how does the voice work? Scientists tell us that speech is produced by vibration of the vocal folds (the modern term for 'vocal cords'), which are two bands of smooth muscle tissue that are opposite each other in the larynx. The larynx is located between the base of the tongue and the top of the trachea, which is the passageway to the lungs.[73]

"When we're not speaking, the vocal folds are open so that we can breathe. When it's time to speak, however, the brain orchestrates a series of events. The vocal folds snap together while air from the lungs blows past, making them vibrate. The vibrations produce sound waves that travel through the throat, nose, and mouth, which act as resonating cavities to modulate the sound. The quality of our voice – its pitch, volume, and tone – is determined by the size and shape of the vocal folds and the resonating cavities. This is why people's voices sound so different."[74]

Can anyone conclude from this that the human being is a product of mere chance?

The glory and power of God is made evident not only by what He has wrought, but in simple fact that we do not fully understand many of the things about the world and about ourselves, despite the numerous scientific developments of the past two hundred years as well as the many astounding technological achievements of recent years that have removed much of their mystery.

One has only to investigate one small aspect of human physiology, such as the immune system, to come away with a deep awe for the marvelous and intricate ways that God has put things together. Also, the mind, which is said to control the inner

---

[73] https//.www.nidcd.nih.gov › health › hoarseness.
[74] Ibid.

workings of the body, including its autonomic or self-regulating systems, is extraordinarily complex. For example, the autonomic systems include those parts of the nervous system that control the muscles of the organs, such as the heart, lungs, stomach, and intestines.

Where does imagination, creativity and inspiration come from? Do we get them from others? Are they inherited?

What gives us memories that cannot be shaken, or longings that must be satisfied? What causes us to hope against hope for a better situation, a better outcome or a better tomorrow, even in the face of imminent danger or the worst of circumstances, or against seemingly stupendous odds?

Can anyone understand everything they do?

The nervous system works through electrical impulses, and some say that all thought is electrical impulses. It's the basis for the science of artificial intelligence. But scientists tell us that they cannot come even close to constructing a complex entity like the human brain, and despite the many technological advancements made in the medical field, including coming up with highly sophisticated imaging and other investigative tools for medical research, no one today understands what makes the brain work. For example, where do thoughts come from? How do they pop into our heads? No one knows.

Physicists have discovered that the apparent solidity of matter is only an illusion. All matter, including the human body, is composed of billions of atoms and molecules, which are 99.99% empty space. The vacuity is unnoticeable to us because it is between the atoms and molecules compared to their size, and there is so much space again within each atom, between the orbiting electrons and the nucleus. But why are things so? No one knows. Perhaps it's just the way things are.

The very best we can do is to try to make sense out of some of these things and use our reason in ways that help us. It is my hope that the information provided in this book will help some of us to do just that. We cannot ensure success at whatever we do, but we can deserve it by doing our best.

All phenomena observed in nature, including the weather, gravity, electricity, chemical reactions and life and death itself, are to some extent mysterious, because Nature does not easily reveal her secrets. Her secrets must be acquired through efforts, by using our minds and abilities to figure out how these things occur so we can use them for our benefit.

But regardless of what our understanding of these things may be, the wonder of nature remains, and, in my opinion, will always remain because man's understanding of his natural world is always limited. Even today, not a single natural phenomenon is fully understood by humankind.

Take, for example, electricity. Nikola Tesla (1856-1943), inventor of the alternating current (AC) motor, believed that electricity came from the air, and that the atmosphere, being electrically charged by the Sun (as evidenced by lightning and the auroras), provides the free electrons. Modern engineers, however, believe that electricity is produced, or generated, by power plants through the action of steam on turbine wheels which spin rotors that are within stators. Tesla knew that you cannot create energy out of nothing, but modern engineers seem to have lost sight of that fact.

Another example is the ever-changing weather. It seems to have a mind of its own. Even with advanced computers supposedly capable of very exacting weather forecasts, predicting the weather is no more of a science today than is fishing, and forecasters are known to be notoriously unreliable.

"In all the things that so great and wise a God has created, there must be many secrets." - St. Teresa of Avila.

In the spring of each year, nature holds up to us a chiding finger reminding us that we are not gods, but over-conceited members of her own great family.

Speaking of the earth and all that God made, Job said:

"But now ask the beasts, and they will teach you; and the birds of the air, and they will tell you. Or speak to the earth, and it will teach you; and the fish of the sea will explain to you. Who among all these does not know that the hand of the Lord has done this, in whose hand is the life of every living thing, and the breath of all mankind?" - Job 12:7-10.

Miracles

We have already seen many of the miracles that God performed in the past. More miracles are discussed herein.

Anyone who has witnessed God's redeeming work in the world, which is perhaps the greatest miracle of all, can testify of the wonderous works of God. As mentioned previously, perhaps the sublimest of miracles is how a human being can love God.

The Scriptures tell us that Jesus' disciples never doubted or questioned Him about the miracles He performed, and neither did His enemies. It seems that one must be removed from that ancient time and place by some 2000 years and several thousand miles, and be well educated, to doubt them.

Miracles are, by definition, surprising events that are not explicable by natural or scientific laws, and are therefore the work of a divine agency.[75]

Miracles happen around us every day that are often overlooked and rarely appreciated. Thoughts control our reality. When we think about miracles, positive thoughts replace negative and troubling thoughts, and the more we think about miracles, the more the many stresses and worries of life diminish in intensity.

There are plenty of miracles to think about.

Creativity is one of the most magical things about life, and one of the most difficult to define because it can be exhibited in so many ways, by artisans, athletes, composers, musicians, carpenters, doctors, lawyers, farmers, plumbers, landscape architects, aircraft designers and the list goes on and on. Webster's dictionary defines it as "the use of the imagination or original ideas, especially in the production of an artistic work." It is the ability to develop new techniques, methods or objects to transcend traditional ways of thinking. We know some of the products or results of creativity, but we do not know how we got it or what its limits are, and it too is something that cannot be given to a machine.

Akin to creativity are imagination and inspiration. They give people ideas and the enthusiasm for developing new things. We know some of the results, but we do not know how we get these abilities, or where they come from. Some believe that instead of

---

[75] Google search for "definition miracle."

being innate qualities like hair or eye color, which are inherited and part of our DNA structure, inspiration flows to us from an external source. Since human experience indicates that a person may be inspired for good or evil purposes, inspiration could come from the devil or God. Billy Graham believed, for example, that Hitler was inspired of the devil. If the inspiration for doing good comes from God, it seems to fit in well with the mystery of life as we know it and with our conception of God as the infinite source of all things.

Consider how clouds can store the essence of hundreds of gallons of water aloft, yet do not fall crashing to the earth. They are amazing wonders of creation. The same goes for the many other marvelous phenomena that make up the natural beauty of the created world.

Photo by the Author.

"He binds up the water in His thick clouds, yet the clouds are not broken under it." - Job 26:8.

Halos

One of the great mysteries of the Bible is the glowing shine of Moses's face when he talked with God (Ex. 34:29-35). As discussed previously, it was so noticeable that it frightened people. Matthew Henry said that serious godliness puts a luster on a man's countenance, but there was more to it than that. It was a most marked change in his appearance, perhaps as striking as the mark of Cain, but of course without its curse (Gen. 4:11-16).

Many Medieval and earlier Christian paintings, stained-glass windows and mosaics depict Jesus and the saints with halos over their heads. Could these depictions be based on fact?

Arnold Ehret, the famous German nutritionist, in his book, *The Cause and Cure of Human Illness*, states that many saints of old were self-radiant due to their ascetic diets and their practice of fasting. Could that also explain Moses' shining face? Or could there more to it? No one knows for sure, but I venture to say that it is the physical manifestation of being exposed for a period of time to the glory of God.

Unseen Forces at Work

Angels are spiritual beings that dwell among the host of heaven that worships God. We commonly know them as God's messengers and servants, who are sent to earth to do His will. They are "ministering spirits" who take delight in their work. They minister to those who are heirs of salvation (Heb. 1:14), i.e., the good seed, not the tares.

The reality of angels coming into this world of time from heaven is described throughout the Bible. It indicates that angels can be visible if they wish to become so. Examples include the angel sent to the parents of Samson, the angel that protected Shadrach, Meshach, and Abed-Nego in the fiery furnace, the angel that protected Daniel in the den of lions, and the angel in human form sent to Zacharias to announce the coming of John the Baptist, and later then to Joseph and, independently, to Mary, the mother of God, who announced the coming of the Lord Jesus Christ.

As discussed previously, an angel freed Peter from prison (Acts 12:5-17).

It is said that everyone has an angel, a guardian angel. The common belief seems to be based on Scripture.

"As Peter knocked at the door of the gate, a girl named Rhoda came to answer. When she recognized Peter's voice, because of her gladness she did not open the gate, but ran in and announced that Peter stood before the gate. But they said to her, "You are beside yourself!" Yet she kept insisting that it was so. So they said, "It is his angel." - Acts 12:13-15.

Jesus' words in Matthew 18:10 seem to support the idea that everyone has a guardian angel. "In heaven their angels always behold the face of my Father who is in Heaven."

David said:

"He will give his angels charge of you to guard you in all your ways. On their hands they will bear you up, lest you dash your foot against a stone" - Ps. 91:11–12.

He also said:

"In all their affliction He was afflicted, and the Angel of His

Presence saved them; in His love and in His pity He redeemed them; and He bore them and carried them all the days of old." - Ps. 63:9.

I have sometimes felt the presence of those who have gone before me who were believers and taught me principles of Christianity. Heb. 12:1 speaks of a great cloud of witnesses referring to the elders whose exhibition of faith obtained a good report. Having borne such witness themselves, they obtained witness from God, and thus became a great cloud of witnesses for our example and encouragement. I believe that Christians have a cloud of witnesses surrounding them that consists not only of the saints of old, but believers who personally knew them in the flesh who have since gone on to live with the Lord. I believe that they help us.

Other than what we have from Scripture, there have been reports by many eye witnesses throughout history of angelic beings assisting mankind. A somewhat recent example is the series of "Apparitions of Our Lady of Fatima" that occurred during the year of 1917.[76] Lucia dos Santos, who was of three children (the eldest, at 10 years of age) to whom the apparitions appeared, eventually became a Carmelite nun, one the strictest orders of nuns.

Thousands of people in the town of Fatima, Portugal witnessed the final apparition on October 13, 1917. Each of the apparitions gave a prediction, and all of them came true.

According to Pope Benedict XVI, they were the most prophetic of all modern apparitions.

---

[76] https://www.americaneedsfatima.org/ANF-Articles/apparitions-of-our-lady-of-fatima.html.

The children saw a lady dressed in white, more brilliant than the sun. According to Lucia, she was Mary, the Mother of God, who, according to Catholic tradition, intercedes for man on behalf of God. She reported that the apparition spoke to them the following words:

"If what I say to you is done, many souls will be saved and there will be peace. The war [World War I] is going to end: but if people do not cease offending God, a worse one will break out during the Pontificate of Pius XI [World War II]. When you see a night illumined by an unknown light, know that this is the great sign given you by God that He is about to punish the world for its crimes, by means of war, famine, and persecutions of the Church and of the Holy Father. To prevent this [World War II], I shall come to ask for the consecration of Russia to my Immaculate Heart, and the Communion of reparation on the First Saturdays. If my requests are heeded, Russia will be converted, and there will be peace; if not, she will spread her errors [Communism] throughout the world, causing wars and persecutions of the Church. The good will be martyred; the Holy Father will have much to suffer; various nations will be annihilated. In the end, my Immaculate Heart will triumph. The Holy Father will consecrate Russia to me, and she shall be converted, and a period of peace will be granted to the world." - Allegedly spoken by the Apparition of Mary, the Mother of God, in the summer of 1917.

Thousands gathered on October 13, 1917 to witness the fourth and final Apparition. A luminous globe was seen to move slowly and majestically through the sky from east to west and then repeated its track in the opposite direction. The Luminosity then spoke to the children. When the conversation ended, Lucia shouted, "Look at the Sun!" The rain stopped, the clouds parted, and the sun appeared as an immense silver disk shining with great intensity. Then the disc began to "dance." It threateningly trembled and shook, and plunged in a zigzag pattern toward the terrified crowd. The apparition was seen by numerous witnesses up to twenty-five miles away from where it took place.[77]

Adela Rodgers St. John, in her book *Tell No Man*, describes how, during the Battle of Britain in 1940, RAF pilots of Hurricanes and Spitfires became either incapacitated or dead, and yet their planes still kept flying and fighting enemy aircraft before safely landing at their airfields. It was confirmed by pilots in the sky and on the ground by groundcrew and other witnesses. Hugh Dowding, the Air Officer Commanding RAF Fighter Command, said that he believed angels had actually flown some of the planes whose pilots sat dead at the controls.

On another occasion, Eddie Rickenbacker, former WWI fighter ace and later Indianapolis Speedway racer, and five other men escaped to the life rafts when their WWII B-17 bomber ran out of fuel and crashed landed in the South Pacific Ocean.

After three weeks adrift without food or water in two cramped rubber life rafts, continually wracked by thirst and hunger and beset by sharks, they decided to split up to improve their chances of rescue.

The raft that was shared by Lieut. Whittaker and Jimmy DeAngelis, who was sick and exhausted, finally approached a small island. But the wind and current were against them.

Whittaker states in his book:[78]

---

[77] Ibid.

[78] Lieut. James C. Whittaker, <u>We Thought We Heard the Angels Sing, The Complete Epic Story of the ordeal and Rescue of Those Who Were with Eddie Rickenbacker on the Plane Lost in the Pacific.</u>

"I have spoken of the rising wind. it brought a deluge of rain that all but blotted out the island. The rain was coming down in torrents. The sharks had doubled in number and appeared to be massing for the attack, whizzing past us and slashing at the oar. I was thoroughly exhausted and there were three weeks of thirst, hunger and suffering behind me. I was calling to God, who alone could save us."

Only a miracle could set their feet on land. Already at strength's end, Whittaker prayed fervently and out loud to God to give him the strength to row against the current using the only thing he had, a small oar that came with the raft. And the miracle came. Somehow, he was able to make it.

"The part of the island where we now stood was only a few hundred feet wide. We were very near the foot. If the Lord hadn't taken hand when He did, we would have missed it entirely and have been out there in the distance somewhere, bound for almost certain death."[79]

If God chooses to do so, He will assist us. "I will be gracious to whom I will be gracious, and I will have compassion on whom I will have compassion." (Ex. 33:19).

In almost all cases of angelic visitation, and in cases where God deigns to step in to assist us in times of need, help comes at the last moment, immediately before all hope is given up. It has been my experience that this is how God chooses to work in our era of dispensation. How wonderful are the merciful dispositions of heaven!

---

[79] Ibid.

Chapter 16 What the Bible Says About the Configuration of the World

It is not the purpose of this book to allay the misgivings of many about their understanding of the world and its configuration, nor to bow to public pressure about them, but to present the Biblical perspective. While aware of the controversial nature of this subject, and that those who say the world is flat not round are heretics, I only wish to present the Bible's side of it. It is up to the reader whether they should take this chapter in tow or disregard it.

We are taught almost from birth that the earth is round in shape, spinning on its axis and orbiting the Sun. No one seems to question it. But what does the Bible say?

According to the Bible, our world is a vast immovable plane, a big, wide world. It never alludes to or suggests anything else. And, many passages of Scripture would not make sense otherwise, as will be discussed. It never describes the world as a planet revolving around the Sun, which, based on the Copernican theory of heliocentrism, together with the belief that since all other worlds we observe by the naked or aided eye are round or spherical in shape then the earth must be that way too. However, the Bible's portrayal of the earth being like a flat dinner plate has never, to my knowledge, been preached or otherwise proclaimed to the church this side of the 16th Century. The church as well as those outside of it have bought in to the global earth theory which is based on so-called proofs and what I call the theology of science.

It is my belief that apart from the divinely inspired Word of God, no theory, no matter how simple or complex it may be, including the theory of the Big Bang, the theory of the origin of the solar system, the theory of evolution, and the global earth theory, can adequately explain the true nature of the world.

Despite its worldwide acceptance, what many people do not realize is that the global earth theory has never been proved. It is based on assumption and speculation. Copernicus himself, who revived the theory of the heathen philosopher Pythagoras, confessed that the system of a revolving earth was only a possibility, and could not be proved by facts.[80]

Even before the American Civil War, most library textbooks had been revised to reflect a round, spinning earth, and since that time almost all books on religion have been similarly revised, with but one exception, the Bible. It alone has remained unaltered.

We are taught throughout our lives to accept the global earth media narrative, which patterns itself after science, without question. And every day, it seems, we hear something new about another scientific discovery that supports or confirms the global earth theory. It has become so much a part of everyday life that it is very difficult for anyone to believe in anything else.

However, when you combine the physics with many commonplace and commonsense observations about the world, some of which are discussed in the subsequent chapter on the Importance of a Worldview, and then consider what the Bible teaches, you find that the actual configuration of the world is as strange and surprising as it is true. I have studied, researched and observed this phenomenon and have seen the many incongruities and inconsistencies that exist in the explanations that modern science has for the nature of the world, including its configuration.

---

[80] David Wardlaw Scott, Terra Firma.

We are increasingly seeing in our culture, and in the world, a general departure from the teachings of the Bible. As mentioned previously, not only are people reading much less today, but fewer are inspired to read the Word of God and find out for themselves what it says about most everything, including the world. As discussed and emphasized throughout this book, the Bible is unquestionably God-breathed and full of high and exquisite wisdom. And, I believe that it can be taken literally.

The following examples illustrate how the Bible describes the configuration of the earth.

"Thus says God, the Lord, who created the heavens and stretched them out, who spread out the earth and what comes from it, who gives breath to the people on it and spirit to those who walk in it." - Isa. 42:5.

He stretched out the heavens and spread out the earth. He spread it out, or spread it forth, as one would spread peanut butter on a slice of bread. He didn't make it into a ball and start it spinning. He spread the earth out.

"Have you comprehended the breadth of the earth? Tell Me, if you know all this." - Job 38:18.

The Book of Isaiah tells us:

"He sits enthroned above the circle of the earth." - Isa. 40:22.

To most people the above verse testifies that the earth is round, since a round earth is depicted in its photos taken from high altitude, and from low earth orbit, as well as those taken from space by the Apollo astronauts, photos which presumably depict a round earth being illuminated by the Sun from 93 million miles away. I was educated as a physicist and trained as an engineer. I understand the scientific point of view and can speak the language.

The above-mentioned verse makes perfect sense if we live on a big, wide or flat earth, for one of the reasons that the photos taken from space are deceptive is that they depict only the portion of the earth being illuminated by the Sun, and it is this "spotlight" coverage of the earth that not only indicates the world we live on is flat, but that the Sun is much smaller and closer to the earth than scientists claim it is. For more information, the reader is kindly referred to the footnoted references on the subject.[81] [82]

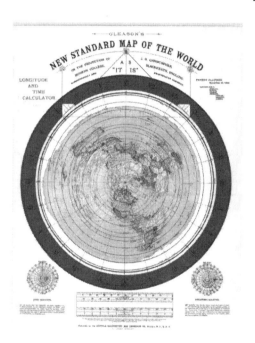

The Gleason Flat Earth Map (scanned by the author).

---

[81] S. H. Shepherd, The Flat Earth Revisited.
[82] Samuel B. Rowbotham, Zetetic Astronomy: Earth Not a Globe.

A map of the flat earth, reproduced above, is available online.[83] It is a faithful representation of how the Bible portrays the world. It depicts a northern center concentric with degrees of latitude. Antarctica is the ring of ice and snow that surrounds the southern circumference. It is the outermost boundary of the circle of the earth. There is no "south pole." Mathematically, the diameter of a flat earth (distance across) is identical to the circumference of a round earth (distance around).[84]

One must also consider the following Bible verses.

"I saw, and behold, a tree in the midst of the earth, and its height was great. The tree grew and became strong, and its top reached to heaven, and it was visible to the end of the whole earth." - Dan. 4:10-11. One could not see a tree reaching to the sky that would be visible to the end of the earth unless the tree was on a big, wide plane.

"And then shall appear the sign of the Son of man in heaven: and then shall all the tribes of the earth mourn, and they shall see the Son of man coming in the clouds of heaven with power and great glory." - Matt. 24:30.

"Behold, He is coming with clouds, and every eye will see Him, even they who pierced Him. And all the tribes of the earth will mourn because of Him." - Rev. 1:7. Everyone on the earth could not see Jesus's second coming unless it could be seen above a flat earth.

---

[83] Flat Earth Map - Gleason's New Standard Map of The World, at https://www.amazon.com/flat-earth-map-Gleasons.
[84] https://wiki.tfes.org /Eratosthenes_on_Diameter.

"Then the devil, taking Him up on a high mountain, showed Him all the kingdoms of the world in a moment of time." - Luke 4:5. Only on a sufficiently high mountain above a flat earth could Jesus view all the kingdoms of the world at one time, since the higher you climb in elevation, the farther into the horizon you can see.

It is noteworthy to mention another teaching of Scripture, which is that someday the stars will fall to the earth. It is a prophesy of Jesus.

"Immediately after the tribulation of those days the Sun will be darkened, and the Moon will not give its light, and the stars will fall from heaven, and the powers of the heavens will be shaken." - Matt. 24:29.

Similar is Isaiah's prophesy:

"All the host of heaven shall be dissolved, and the heavens shall be rolled up like a scroll. All their host shall fall down as the leaf falls from the vine, and as fruit falling from a fig tree." - Isa. 34:4.

It is also in the Book of Revelation:

"And the stars of the sky fell to the earth as the fig tree sheds its winter fruit when shaken by a gale." - Rev. 6:13:

These verses affirm that the stars are placed in the firmament, and furthermore, that they will fall to the earth.

Stars falling from heaven would not be possible on an insignificant speck of dust drifting in the immensity of the postulated universe. Nevertheless, most people would rather believe public opinion than the Bible, for they fear public opinion more than they do the Bible.

When presented with the case that the Bible teaches a flat, immovable plane earth and not what they thought it was, accepting such a belief would mean reappraising many things that have been taken for granted for far too long. It would point out man's fallibility for believing in a lie. It would upset an enormous number of things. In fact, a shift in worldview of such magnitude would cause worldwide upheaval.

It would mean an end to the sense of security that people have about what is said to be true about the world. It would have profound and far-reaching implications for everyone. Its revolutionary impact on the world would, perhaps, be equivalent to that made by Jesus, Himself.

"There are a great many theories about how the world began, but all of them can be boiled down to fit into a twofold classification: one is creation, and the other is speculation. All theories fall into one of these two divisions." - J. Vernon McGee.

Many people have tried to rationalize the creation account to make it fit in with global earth theory, but they have never been able to do so because of the many differences that would have to be reconciled.

Because science cannot prove the existence of God, or any other supernatural entity, it cannot admit of the possibility of the supernatural. Denouncing the Bible as old school and irrelevant to modern times, scientists claim that they alone know the truth about the origin of all things.

"Science has closed our eyes and thrown us into an abyss of ignorance about the few things that really matter." - Paul Tillich.

Chapter 17 Our Conduct

"I am Almighty God; walk before Me and be blameless." - Gen. 17:1.

How should we conduct ourselves in the world? Should we tolerate evil or oppose it? What do the Scriptures say? These and other topics are explored in this chapter.

Numerous books have been written on the subject of Christian conduct. It's as though many Christians feel that they must justify their actions, and it seems that everyone has an opinion on what makes a good Christian. But from my experience, much of what is said is pious, uninspired and repetitious commentary, written to impress rather than convince, or published for reasons that have more to do with advancing one's prestige in the church than anything else.

The Bible teaches that God has expectations for man, and especially for Christians. After He gives us a measure of His Spirit, He expects us to carry much of the brunt of the work that He wants done in the world in fulfilment of His purposes. The Bible tells us what these purposes are. However, because everyone is given only a portion of the Spirit (Acts 2:38), one deemed by Him to be fitting for them to have, His purposes are accomplished in us in different ways.

God is a God of variety, as evidenced by the many different species of plants and animals on the earth, by the many stars in the heavens, each of which have a different glory (1 Cor. 15:41), and are called by different names (Ps. 147:4), and by the differences that are evident in each one of us, for each of us is unique from the rest, having been born unique.

Christians are the salt of the earth (Matt. 5:13), a purifying influence in the world, preventing the rottenness of the world from corrupting everything in it. As discussed in the chapter on the Spirit of God, the Bible tells us that it is what the Holy Spirit does through us, and what He does on His own, that restrains the powers of evil from taking over the world.

Do Not Repay Evil, But Oppose It

One of the most prevalent stumbling stones and rocks of offense in the church today is its position on evil. I could say it is *the* stumbling stone and rock of offense. Many churches have already, and others show signs that they soon will, depart from the fundamentals of the faith by endorsing immoral practices, including homosexuality in its members. Many have held conferences on the need to change their mission statements to allow these deviations from past church principles. It is partly the result of many laws that have been passed in recent years permitting same-sex marriage and divorce due to the political weight of public opinion that holds sway in our permissive society. It is also due in part to the well-recognized decline in church attendance and its corresponding loss of monetary contributions. Nevertheless, its prevalence is growing and it's not just local but worldwide in scope.

Many verses of the Bible condemn homosexuality as a sin (for example, Lev. 18:13 and 20:13, Rom. 1:26-27, 1 Cor. 6:9-10, 1 Tim. 1:10, Gen. 19:5, Deut. 22:5, Judges 19:22 and 1 Kings 14:24), and God hates sin (Ps. 5:5, Ps. 11:5, Ps. 34:16, Ps. 101:3, Prov. 6:16-19, and Zech. 8:17). It is an abomination to God and should not be condoned by the church. He will punish those who practice it.

Christianity has always been unconventional, and opposed to

accepted behavior. Jesus was unconventional. It was seen in many of His ways, including emphasizing the spirit versus letter of the law and making the tax collector Matthew one of his disciples.

"Blessed is the man who walks not in the counsel of the ungodly, nor stands in the path of sinners, nor sits in the seat of the scornful; but his delight is in the law of the Lord, and in His law he meditates day and night. He shall be like a tree planted by the rivers of water, that brings forth its fruit in its season, whose leaf also shall not wither; and whatever he does shall prosper. The ungodly are not so, but are like the chaff which the wind drives away. Therefore, the ungodly shall not stand in the judgment, nor sinners in the congregation of the righteous. For the Lord knows the way of the righteous, but the way of the ungodly shall perish." - Ps. 1:1-6.

Jesus did say, " I tell you not to resist an evil person. But whoever slaps you on your right cheek, turn the other to him also." (Matt.5:39). It was spoken in the context of the law of Moses. He does not repeal that law, which was meant for the judges of Israel to impose, but the Jews had extended it to private conduct, and made it the rule by which to take revenge. We are to suffer any injury that can be born, but: "Take no part in the unfruitful works of darkness, but instead expose them." (Eph. 5:11). "Resist the devil, and he will flee from you." (James 4:7).

We are to repay no one evil for evil (Prov. 20, 22, 1 Pet. 3:9, Rom. 12:17-21), for it enlarges the evil and is unhealthy to boot, but we are to admonish evildoers for their evil (Rom. 12:17). All of Scripture must be used to rightly divide Word of truth (2 Tim. 2:15).

Jesus was no non-contesting Gautama Buddha. He tolerated no unjust or unrighteous thing, and we are to be like Him if we want

176

to be His followers (Matt. 5:13-16). We are to make a difference in the world – preach the Word in season and out of season, correct, rebuke and encourage with great patience those who are seeking the truth.

"Righteousness exalts a nation, but sin condemns any people." - Prov. 14:34.

"If then the light in you is darkness, how great is the darkness!" - Matt. 6:23.

The Bible teaches heterosexuality not homosexuality (Gen 1:28, Gen. 9:7, Mal. 2:5, Eph. 5:22-33). Those in the church who preach a gospel different than that of the Bible are outsiders who have crept in unnoticed, who long ago were designated for this condemnation; ungodly people, who pervert the grace of our God into sensuality (Jude 1:4). The stumbling stone of tolerance and permissiveness that is widely exhibited in the church today will fall on it and crush it if it does not repent.

"Everyone then who hears these words of Mine and acts on them will be like a wise man who built his house on rock... and everyone who hears these words of Mine and does not act on them will be like a foolish man who built his house on the sand." - Matt. 7:24-26.

Pious teachings of the church throughout the ages, and especially today, encourage Christians to be tolerant of others, to accept what they do, and be docile creatures who mind their own business. It is partly based on an incorrect application of Scripture, namely 1 Thess. 4:11-12, which says, "And to aspire to live quietly, and to mind your own affairs, and to work with your hands, as we instructed you, so that you may walk properly before outsiders and be dependent on no one." In order to rightly interpret Scripture, it is sometimes necessary to look at the overall context of a verse or passage. In this case, Paul is asking members of the Church of Thessalonica to cease meddling in the affairs of the brothers and sisters in Christ. It is not meant to encourage Christians to be tolerant of those outside the church.

The same is true of the verse excerpt, "Give no offense." (1 Cor. 10:32). The entire verse is, "Give no offense, either to the Jews or to the Greeks or to the church of God." It means that we should give no offense to those who are true believers and abide in Christ, or to those who may be converted to the faith who should be treated as objects of Christian solicitude. It does not mean that we should tolerate and refrain from opposing evil in our midst.

The Bible teaches that there is righteous anger, which is anger against evil. Our feelings are not wrong when they are directed to their legitimate object. Wrath is forbidden, but anger not so. Anger itself in man is not sin, for our Lord Himself felt it (Mark 3:5, John 2:15), and none of us should be confused about the matter.

Our Response

Orderly, peaceful living is one of the virtues of life, and especially Christian life. We should be diligent and productive workers for God and seek the peaceful life, and expect the same of others. It does not mean, however, that we should have no say in the ongoing battle against the forces of good and evil. On the contrary, we are to speak out against evil and insist that justice be done (Lev. 19:17). Instead of joining forces with the world, we are to make a difference in the world.

If a wrong has been committed or is being fostered by men, or when the rights of others, or our rights, are infringed upon, we are to stand up and be counted.   We are to let our righteousness, our ability to discern between good and evil, shine forth to the world. We are to challenge others when they are going astray and when they are wrong – when they do not do what is right. It is what God intends to be accomplished by His representatives in the world.

Many of the Quakers, perhaps the most famous being William Penn, have advocated avoiding company where it is not profitable or necessary, and where it is necessary to speak little and last. It is well-spoken advice, but another aspect of proper Christion behavior is to confront evil.

We are to oppose evil in all of its forms and make a difference in the world.

As stated in the chapter on Division, a Christian is a separated man. He is separated forever unto God. He stands alone in the world and is set apart from others to serve the purposes of God. We are the light of the world, shining our light into its darkness, and Jesus told us to let our light shine before others (Matt. 5:16).

If we see evil in the world, we should oppose it. If we doubt the motivations of others, we should challenge them, and back it up with Scripture.

How Jesus Responded to Evil

When Jesus was brought before Annas for questioning and was asked about His disciples and His doctrine, he replied, "I spoke openly to the world. I always taught in synagogues and in the temple, where the Jews always meet, and in secret I have said nothing. Why do you ask Me? Ask those who have heard what I said to them. Indeed they know what I said." (John 18:20-21). When He was slapped by one of the officers who said, "Do You answer the high priest like that?", Jesus answered him, "If I have spoken evil, bear witness of the evil; but if well, why do you strike Me?" He did not use violence and strike back, but He stood up to them and confronted their evil abuse.

Other examples of where Jesus opposed his adversaries by confronting and correcting them include the following:

- When He healed the man with the withered hand (Matt. 12:9-21, Mark 3:1-6, Luke 6:6-11).

- When they brought to Him a woman caught in adultery (John 8:1-11).

- When He called the scribes and Pharisees hypocrites, blind guides, serpents, brood of vipers, and sons of hell (Matt. 15:7-8, Matt. 23:13-36, John 8:37-47).

- When He corrected and admonished the Pharisees about divorce (Matt. 19:1-6), and the Sadducees about the living God being the God of the resurrected (Matt. 22:23-33).

- When He cleansed the temple (Matt. 21:12-17, John 2:13-22).

More examples of where Jesus confronted and corrected his adversaries are discussed in the next chapter, including the parable of the *Wedding Feast* and the parable of the *Ten Minas*. There were also times when Jesus confronted and corrected his own disciples, such as when He admonished Peter who forbade Him to allow the Jews to kill Him (Matt. 16:21-23), and when Peter boldly proclaimed that he would die for Him, Jesus told him that he would deny Him three times that night before the cock crowed (Matt. 26:34, Mark 14:30).

From these examples, and more, we learn what we ought to do when confronted with evil, how we should stand up for ourselves and others and admonish those who do evil.

"Through Your precepts I get understanding; therefore I hate every false way." - Ps. 119:104.

We are not to mimic or reflect the rudeness or callousness of others, but be examples to them of wholeness, integrity and discipline. We do this by mimicking what Jesus would do in our place, realizing all the while the temporary nature of the world. Life is short, and if you disbelieve it then you will certainly agree that it is very short comparted to eternity. We're only here for a little while to do the best we can, and then we are gone.

Christian Maturity

We are daily being transformed into the nature of Jesus Christ by the ministering power of the Holy Spirit. We grow through the Spirit. We cannot mature as Christians on our own. The process is accomplished through prayer and the amount of time we spend in the Word ("To the teaching and to the Testimony!" - Isa. 8:20), weighing precept upon precept, line upon line (Isa. 28:10), and as we practice being more like Jesus.

However, many Christians spend very little, if any, time in the Holy Scriptures. They must feign familiarity with what Jesus taught. They also spend very little time in prayer. The most common complaint is that they do not have time for these things. Furthermore, many of the things Christians read, listen to and watch are without redeeming value. But salvation is not something to be taken lightly, for it was purchased at a very high price, the precious blood of Christ on the Cross. How would you feel if you received little or no respect or gratitude for saving someone's life?

Man is basically superstitious, and, without the Word of God, he remains superstitious. When Peter took his eyes off Jesus, he began to sink beneath the waves (Matt. 14:30). When John and his brother James put their desires above their duty, they got their mother to ask Jesus if they could sit beside Him, one on the left and one on the right, in His kingdom (Matt. 20:20-21, Mark 20:35-37).

Many Christians do not mature in the ways that God wants them to, but remain as babes in Christ, infants in Christ. They are Sunday Christians who have no interest in the Bible. They give up trying to be like the Master, and cease doing good works. Others study the Word and grow. They want to be more like Jesus, they want to learn more about Him, so they press on and strive to be more like Him (Hos. 6:3). Maturity is reached when Jesus becomes a Christian's constant friend and companion. Life then is full of joy and fun and exciting, for you never know what He will do through you next. The Christian maturing process never ceases, for the longer one knows Christ, the more one matures and the more fruitful they become.

Christ in Us

The Bible teaches that when the Holy Spirit dwells in us, we are spiritually illumined, and know that Jesus is in us (John 14:20, 1 John 3:24). How do we know? Our unseen Lord is known by His Word, by the Holy Spirit, by answered prayer, by the many blessings He bestows on us, by what He has created, and by the circumstances He sometimes works in our favor. The more we know Him, the more our faith is increased, and a strong faith in Him is what pleases God more than anything else (Heb. 11:6, John 20:29, 1 Pet. 1:7-8). The more we abide in Him, the more certain we are that He is in us. He is a very gentle leader, and the more we abide in Him the more sensitive we are of his light hand.

We are temples in which He dwells, and as we abide in Him, He makes Himself at home in us. It means continual house cleaning, rearranging and modifying but it also means continual revelation, continuing to receive insights about Him.

"To live in Christ is to live in a mystery equal to that of the Incarnation and similar to it. For as Christ unites in His one Person the two natures of God and of man, so too in making us His friends He dwells in us, uniting us ultimately with Himself. Dwelling in us He becomes as it were our superior self, for He has united and identified our inmost self with Himself." - Thomas Merton, *New Seeds of Contemplation*.

You come to realize that it is not what you do any longer but what He does through you.

"You are no longer strangers and foreigners, but fellow citizens with the saints and members of the household of God, having been built on the foundation of the apostles and prophets, Jesus Christ Himself being the chief cornerstone, in whom the whole building, being fitted together, grows into a holy temple in the Lord, in whom you also are being built together for a dwelling place of God in the Spirit." - Eph. 2:19-22.

You soon begin to have communion (or union) with God in His way, for He leads you in that direction. When this occurs, it is important to engage in contemplative prayer, a form of prayer discussed in the chapter on the Spirit of God. It helps put aside many thoughts that can creep in and interfere with prayer. We learn through practice to shut them out, for this form of prayer is a union with God as we focus our thoughts not on ourselves but on Him. It is accomplished by repeating, in the mind, a loving word or statement of something you feel is true about Him. A goodness descends from on high, and stays with us, which changes our thoughts and dreams, making them wholesome and sweet instead of unhealthy, confused or wearisome. Good things once taken for granted become prized. Things about your life that have always bothered you, that have broken your sleeps and given you bad dreams, become resolved because you realize at last why they occurred and why you acted the way you did.

And it is when we love Him that we will share Him with others.

The Virtue of Humility

One of the most important qualities of Christians is, or should be, humility, a modest or low view of one's own importance. It has always been the mark of a true believer, for it is obtained through the Spirit of God. No one will make it to heaven who has not humbled themselves at the foot of the Cross.

Before being saved, we are full of pride, thinking we are something. When saved, we realize our helpless, vile and wretched condition before a holy God, which is our true condition in the world.

"Humility is nothing else but a man's true understanding of himself as he really is. It is certain that if a man could truly see and be conscious of himself as he really is, he would, indeed, be truly humble." - Author (anonymous) of *The Cloud of Unknowing*.

Humility is giving thanks, knowing that we do not deserve what is given to us. Humility and faith are the cornerstones of Christianity. God treasures those who have a humble and contrite spirit (Isa. 66:2, Ps. 34:18, Ps. 51:17), and instructs the humble in His way (Ps. 25:9).

Humility allows one to treat others more important than themselves and refrain from a quick judgment of others. We are to be severe on our own faults, but charitable in our judgement of others, and this we do when we have the humility of the Bible.

Two worldly examples of humility are seen in Sir Isaac Newton and Thomas Edison:

"I am as a child on the seashore picking up a pebble here and a shell there, but the great ocean of truth still lies before me." - Sir Isaac Newton.

"I do not know one millionth part of one percent about anything." - Thomas Edison.

A good example of humility in the Bible is David after he was made king.

"King David went in and sat before the Lord and he said, "Who am I, O Lord God, and what is my house that You have brought me this far?" - 2 Sam. 7:18.

David also said,

"Lord, make me to know my end, and what is the measure of my days, that I may know how frail I am." - Ps. 39:4.

Again, David, who was said to be a man after God's own heart (Acts 13:21-23, 1 Sam. 13:14):

"I am poor and needy; yet the Lord thinks upon me." - Ps. 40:17.

The best example of humility, however, is Jesus. He was of humble origin and was born in a stable (Luke 2:7). His mother and foster father were common people of no reputation, as exemplified not only by His birth in a stable but by their sacrifice of a pair of turtledoves, or two young pigeons, at the time of Mary's purification (Luke 2:22). He made Himself of no reputation, and His appearance was like that of any other man (Phil. 2:7). He was Lord of Lords and King of Kings (1 Tim. 6:15), but He took upon Him the form of a servant. He surrounded Himself with humble fishermen and those who had humbled themselves before God. He cured the sick and asked for nothing in return. He humbled Himself more than any other man by being obedient to the point of death, even the death of the Cross (Phil. 2:8).

As exemplified in Jesus, humility does not mean fearfulness or timidity, and it certainly does not mean that we should refrain from challenging those who are in the wrong, for there are times when we need to stand up for our rights and those of others.

One of the values of humility is found on the job. It shouldn't be confused with a desire to achieve and obtain good performance marks; rather, it is having and showing due respect for those we live and work with, and those that hire us, for respect of others is something our Lord expects us to exhibit. It is treating others more important than ourselves.

"Let nothing be done through selfish ambition or conceit, but in lowliness of mind let each esteem others better than himself." - Phil. 2:3.

"Talk no more so very proudly; let no arrogance come from your mouth, for the Lord is the God of knowledge; and by Him actions are weighed." - 1 Sam. 2:3.

Again, denying ourselves and esteeming others better than ourselves does not mean that we shouldn't oppose evil whenever we see it. This is another stumbling block for many Christians which reduces their effectiveness in the world, for when we face evil we do not face it alone, but have the strength of the supernatural power of the Holy Spirit to confront it with us (2 Tim. 1:7).

Covetousness

"Let your conduct be without covetousness; be content with such things as you have. For He Himself has said, "I will never leave you nor forsake you." - Heb. 13:5.

Covetousness, which is an inordinate desire for wealth or possessions, is closely related to envy, which is one of the seven deadly sins of the Catholic Church. It is a desire to possess a greater portion of worldly goods than God has given us, and it is closely related to ambition.

The tenth commandment of God is, "Thou shalt not covet." (Ex. 20:17, Deut. 5:21). We are not to covet because it is a sin against God, but another reason is provided in First Timothy:

"Those who want to get rich fall into temptation and a snare and many foolish and harmful desires which plunge men into ruin and destruction. For the love of money is a root of all sorts of evil, and some by longing for it have wandered away from the faith and pierced themselves with many griefs." - 1 Tim. 6:9-10.

Note that it does not say, those that are rich, but those who want to get rich, those who put the quest for riches above all else in life, and place all their happiness in worldly wealth. Money is not the root of all evil, but the love of it is. People may have money and not love it, but if they love it, it will drive them to do evil, which will find itself out (Num. 32:23) and increase their sorrow.

It is an admonition that should be taken to heart, for fame and riches are what most people value above all else. In God's view, however, everything we have was given to us, for we brought nothing into this world and it is certain that we shall carry nothing out (1 Tim. 6:7, Ps. 49:17). Everything we have is on loan to us, and we are its caretakers until the day of our departure, when we must relinquish it all. Meanwhile, we are expected to be trustworthy stewards of what we possess, for He will demand an account of it.

"You shall not have in your bag differing weights, a heavy and a light. You shall not have in your house differing measures, a large and a small. You shall have a perfect and just weight, a perfect and just measure, that your days may be lengthened in the land which the Lord your God is giving you. For all who do such things [cheat in business], all who behave unrighteously, are an abomination to the Lord your God." - Deut. 25: 13-16.

When we buy or sell, when we do business of any kind, we should conduct ourselves as though He was watching us, for He is watching us. We learned from the last chapter that God is omnipresent. His eyes go throughout the world and observe everything. We should be honest in all our transactions, stealing nothing and cheating no one.

If we are faithful in what is least, we will be counted faithful in what is much, but if we are unfaithful in what is least, we will be counted unfaithful also in much (Luke 16:10-12). This is a great moral principle.[85]

How do we find contentment in this life? Paul tells us where it is to be found, in living a God-filled life (for example, Heb. 13:5 and 1

---

[85] Most supervisors and managers are familiar with this principle.

Tim 6:7-8). Contentment overrules the evils of covetousness. If we are content with what we have, we will not be susceptible to covetousness.

Faith

Faith is the sum and substance of the Christian life. A child of God is known by his or her faith in God's illustrious Son. Though we cannot peer into God's abode, faith, the "substance of things hoped for, the evidence of things not seen" (Heb. 11:1), gives us the possession of those eternal things now, and makes them exert their power with us in our walk with God. In Scripture, "walk" means the daily conduct of a man here on earth. "We walk by faith, not by sight." - 2 Cor. 5:7. Faith is the opposite of sight.

If we have faith and do not doubt, we have the support of the Lord (Matt. 21:21, Mark 11: 3-24, James 1:5-8, 1 Pet. 1:8), which assures us that our prayers will be answered (John 16:23-24).

Many people believe in a supreme being, or entity, that is behind all things, and that nature is the product of a designing intelligence, but that it is no longer active in the world. Many people in the past believed it, and the same is true today. But it falls short of the teachings of the Bible. It is the concept of God that depicts Him as a great watchmaker who made the world and put it in motion but then left to let it run on its own. It is a concept that assumes He is no longer here, but the Bibles teaches that God is omnipresent, that his eyes run forth throughout the world (2 Cor. 16:9).

Merely believing in God is not sufficient, for even the demons believe, and tremble (James 2:19). A person can believe that there is, or must be, a God, but it will not pay their admittance to heaven, and neither will good works without faith.

Many people say that they will believe it if they see it. It was the same among the disciples of Christ, who saw and heard Him every day. One day they asked Him to increase their faith (Luke 17:5). He replied:

"If you have faith as small as a mustard seed, you can say to this mulberry tree, 'Be uprooted and planted in the sea,' and it will obey you." - Matt. 17:6.

Later Phillip, speaking for the disciples who had doubts about who Jesus was, said:

"Lord, show us the Father, and it is sufficient for us.' Jesus said to him, 'Have I been with you so long, and yet you have not known Me, Philip? He who has seen Me has seen the Father; so how can you say, 'Show us the Father'? Do you not believe that I am in the Father, and the Father in Me? The words that I speak to you I do not speak on My own authority; but the Father who dwells in Me does the works." (John 14:8-9).

The disciples were slow to believe and slow to understand what Jesus said and did. Nevertheless, Jesus was patient with them, as He is with every generation, for He wishes that no one should perish but that all should come to repentance and be saved.

God gives us troubles to test our faith. He puts us through the fire to test our mettle. He wants us to be more like His Son, who trusted God even to the point of death on the Cross.

As previously discussed, we are tempered by trials and sufferings. Although it may feel like we're being forged in the fire, it is God's way of strengthening us through the filling up of the sufferings of Christ and the testing of our faith (Col. 1:24, James 1:3, 1 Pet. 1:7). Also, as stated previously, God indeed tests our faith and chastens those whom He loves. But chastening can take on many forms, and perhaps each is chosen to have a unique effect on the individual's growth and well-being, in material as well as spiritual ways.

We have only to look to the Scriptures to see a shining example of where faith was strongly tested, and never more triumphantly stood the test. It was when God commanded Abraham to sacrifice his son, Isaac (Gen. 22:2-14). It shows the close relationship that faith shares with hope. God had told Abraham that it would be through Isaac that his descendants would be multiplied as the sand on the seashore and as the stars in heaven, and that through his seed the whole world would be blessed. Yet, Abraham was at the point of thrusting the knife into his son before he was stopped by an angel of God. Hebrews 11:19 tells us that Abraham's faith was so strong that he knew God could, and would if necessary, raise Isaac from the dead to fulfill His Word.

All true Christians are endued with the miracle of faith. They are justified by faith (Rom. 5:1). Faith is what purifies the heart of corruption (Acts. 15:9).

Faith is one of the keys to heaven, and without it no one can get in. God told us at the Mount of Transfiguration (Luke 9:35) concerning Jesus, "Listen to Him!" An analogous exhortation would be, "Have faith in Him!"

Of all the graces that are so kindly bestowed on us by the Holy Spirit, faith, hope and love are the most important (1 Cor. 13:13), for they endure forever, being imperishable and immortal. The world and the church will pass away when the perfect succeeds the imperfect, but faith, hope and love will remain in the next life, exalted and purified.

Fruit

Fruit is the outgrowth perfection of a mature plant, whether it be a bush, tree or some other plant. It represents the intended purpose for which the plant was created.

The fruit of the Spirit is spiritual fruit that is given to a person when he or she repents of their sins and accepts the truth about Jesus Christ. It is described in Gal. 5:22-23. Without Jesus, we can produce no such fruit.

It is the spiritual Vine, not the branches, that produces the fruit of the Spirit (John 15:5). Jesus is the gardener, the cultivator, the one who cares for his "trees," providing them with the living water and fertilizer of His Word.

Although a Christian may receive some of the fruits, as well as some of the gifts of the Spirit at the time of rebirth, and/or when they minister to others in charitable ways, it has been my experience that the more time spent in the Word of God, the more fruit is produced, since abiding in His Word is tantamount to abiding in the Vine.

Many of us are slow to learn, including myself. It usually takes me two or three times at anything before I can figure out how to do it. The more truths that are reiterated, the more they are internalized and made our own. Dawn to sunrise can take a while; a single coat of paint is typically not enough, for it soon rubs off.

The Lord knew this about people because He knows all about people. It is why He repeated many of His miracles and teachings before the crowds and His disciples. The four Gospels present His miracles and teachings in slightly different forms and content because He repeated them often. As a performer who speaks often in public, or an entertainment group that performs their repertoire for different audiences, our Lord slightly modified His words and healed the sick in slightly different ways the more often He repeated them. The disciples were slow to learn, as we hear Jesus tell them repeatedly. I am of the opinion that He repeated His miracles and teachings for their sake, so that they would better remember them.

Our reading of the Word should be more than a ritual, for we need the living water and fertilizer of the Word to make us grow. The branch is nourished most that continually receives the sap of the vine. God desires communion with us, and it is accomplished through persistent time spent in the Word. "Herein is My Father glorified, that ye bear much fruit." (John 15:8).

Birds, fish and other animals know what they were created to do, for it is what they must do, but man questions why and for what reason he lives, and seldom discovers the answer. Thank God for religion, that can lead man to do what he was created to do – understand God and have fellowship with Him.

Duty

To love God is the sum of a man's duty and the beginning of all goodness. When we love God, we will glorify Him and fulfill His purpose in creating us. This was discussed in the chapter on Suffering. The Westminster Shorter Catechism,[86] written in 1646, says:

"The chief end of man is to glorify God and enjoy Him forever."

When we love God, it makes everything we do more worthwhile.

---

[86] A catechism is a summary or exposition of Christian doctrine.

It should be total and undivided love, but just about any kind of love for God separates us from others because it makes us different, as Jesus' message on division (Luke 12:49-53) tells us. The separation is good for us while it may be bad for others, but it may seem bad for us because we no longer act like they do. "Thou shalt love the Lord thy God with all thy heart, and with all thy soul, and with all thy mind. This is the first and great commandment. And the second is like unto it, thou shalt love thy neighbor as thyself." (Matt. 22:37-40, Mark 12:30, Luke 10:27, Deut. 6:5). Obeying this injunction is much harder than it may at first seem, but it is what God expects us to do.

The second part of the injunction is that we shall love our neighbor, our fellowman, as ourselves. It may seem like a shared love between God and man, but John teaches that it isn't the case at all, for the love of man springs from the love of God (1 John 4:7). Therefore, the two are one and inseparable. Our neighbor, as explained in the parable of the Good Samaritan (Luke 10:25-37), is anyone who is in want, who is in need.

Jesus said that it is better to give than to receive (Acts 20:35). This divine law is directly opposed to man's natural way of thinking. But Christianity is not a natural religion. There is nothing natural about it. It is supernatural within and without. It comes right from heaven and is the divine outflow of the crucified and risen Son of God. No other religion on earth has the hope, the umbrella of protection, the consciousness or the power that Christianity has.

When you love God, you will love your neighbor, and from then on everything flows sweetly, for you will treat others as you wish to be treated (Matt. 7:12), but not like the world treats others – in ways that sustain a live-and-let-live philosophy (I'll let you do your thing if you let me do mine) – but in ways that are esteemed in the sight of God.

We cannot be effective Christians without prayer, for God accomplishes more through us than we are able to accomplish on our own. Until a Christian matures and starts praying unceasingly, I recommend prayer be offered at least twice a day, once in the morning and once in the evening, for God commanded Israel to sacrifice a lamb along with the grain and drink offering once in the morning and once at twilight (Ex. 29:38-39), and prayer is our sacrifice to God (Ps. 51:17).

Forgiveness is a duty (Matt. 6:15, Mark 11:25, Eph. 4:32), but like love, it also springs from God. When we dwell on how God has forgiven our sins, our trespasses against Him, we reciprocate by forgiving others their trespasses against us. But without God's love and forgiveness, this is not possible.

The Lord's prayer reminds us of the need to forgive others. "Give us this day our daily bread, and forgive us our trespasses as we forgive those who trespass against us." (Matt. 6:11-12, NKJV). Most of the translations use the word "debt" for "trespass," but it is often interpreted literally when it ought to be figuratively. With today's great emphasis on the importance of money, the use of "debt" in the prayer seems to imply that if others are not indebted to us monetarily or in some other material way, then we are not required to forgive them. But that is not what Jesus was talking about.

As there is no limit to the number of sins that God cannot forgive in us, there should be no limit to the number of times we should forgive others (Matt. 18:21-22). Every time we do not forgive the trespasses of others is a non-fulfilment of Christian duty.

The duty of Christians is to do God's bidding as bondservants of Christ, and serve Him in the ways that He wants to be served.

Duty has a sense of timing associated with it. In the case of forgiveness, we are to do it promptly (Mark 11:25, Matt. 5:25-26). We are, after all, only a vapor that appears for a little while and then vanishes, and none of us knows when our vanishing will occur (Job 14:1-2, Ps. 39:4-6, Ps. 144:4, James 4:14). It puts on us the onus to act with presence of mind. We are not to put off for tomorrow what can be done today.

"Only fear the Lord and serve Him in truth with all your heart; for consider what great things He has done for you." - 1 Sam. 12:24.

Our proper attitude toward God at the end of each day is shown by what Jacob said in Gen. 32:10 on his journey away from his brother-in-law Laban: "I am not worthy of the least of all the mercies and of all the truth which You have shown Your servant." It is also reflected in what Jesus told his disciples about the dutiful servant in the Book of Luke:

"And which of you, having a servant plowing or tending sheep, will say to him when he has come in from the field, 'Come at once and sit down to eat'? But will he not rather say to him, 'Prepare something for my supper, and gird yourself and serve me till I have eaten and drunk, and afterward you will eat and drink'? Does he thank that servant because he did the things that were commanded him? I think not. So likewise you, when you have done all those things which you are commanded, say, 'We are unprofitable servants. We have done what was our duty to do." - Luke 17:7-10.

Obedience to God's Word often brings us into difficult places. When God commanded Abraham to leave the Ur of the Chaldeans, the land of his fathers, and go to the land of Canaan, many troubles befell him, including famine (Gen. 12:10) and the hatred of others (Gen. 26:19), but they resulted in blessings bestowed on him and those who were with him. When Isaac was told by God not to go down to Egypt but stay in the land of Canaan, he also had many troubles, but God blessed him bountifully (Gen. 26:2-4). Same with Moses when God sent him to Pharaoh to ask for the release of Israel from his land (Ex. 3:7-31). First Kings tells us that not one word failed of all the good promises that God gave to Israel (1 Kings 8:56).

When David slew Goliath and became the champion of Israel, he encountered the wrath and envy of the king, who from then on tried to kill him in order that he might remain king. David was forced to live in the wilderness for years until Saul died in battle on Mt. Gilboa, but he then became King David. When Cyrus king of Persia, in fulfilment of prophesy, proclaimed in writing throughout his kingdom that He would rebuild the temple of God at Jerusalem, and that the Jews which were left in his kingdom were free to go back to Jerusalem and build it, they suffered from all sides during its construction, but it was through them that the Messianic prophesy was later fulfilled (Hag. 2:23, Matt. 1:12-13, Luke 3:27).

When the disciples left everything at Jesus' bidding to follow Him, they lived in want and austerity, but received a hundredfold in this life and in the age to come eternal life (Mark 10:30).

In each case, a divine law appears to be in effect: that God blesses those who do His will, but only after they do His will, and despite the sufferings that may be experienced in the process.

197

"Has the Lord as great delight in burnt offerings and sacrifices as in obeying the voice of the Lord? Behold, to obey is better than sacrifice, and to heed than the fat of rams." - 1 Sam. 15:22.

As discussed previously, we are to stand up for right and oppose what is wrong in the world. It is our duty, and, if we have the faith of a mustard seed we will perform it. We are to be bold to oppose what we perceive as wrong in the world.

Jesus was sent at a time when everything He did, whether it was preaching the Word or performing miracles, was opposed by the religious rulers of His people, and His own did not receive Him. But as many as received Him, He gave the right to become children of God (John 1:10-12). It was a time which seemed the most conducive to conflict and the least to acceptance, but we are told that to God it was the acceptable time (Gal. 4:4-5).

Reading the Bible

We are to read the Bible. The first Psalm states:

"Blessed is the man who walks not in the counsel of the ungodly or stands in the path of sinners, nor sits in the seat of the scornful, but his delight is in the law of the Lord, and in His law he meditates day and night." - Ps. 1:1-2.

It is written in the Book of Joshua:

"This Book of the Law shall not depart from your mouth, but you shall meditate in it day and night, that you may observe to do according to all that is written in it. For then you will make your way prosperous, and then you will have good success." - Josh. 1:8.

I have always adhered to this injunction, reading the Bible twice daily, once in the morning and once in the evening, because I believe it. Its message is quite different from the false-prosperity message given to us by many in the church that says that a person will receive riches and blessings in this life just by giving generously to some ministry or by doing certain good works.

Reverence for God's Word

Christians are to defend the creeds of the church and devote their lives to its preservation. We are not to speak of the Holy Scriptures or make reference to them in a careless or offhanded manner. If we do so, we break the third commandment of God and take His name in vain. We are to affirm the authority of the Scriptures and champion its absolute truths against skeptical viewpoints.

The inviolability and integrity of the Scriptures has been, and continues to be, the most time-tested and inescapable truth of all history. The words of the Bible are from the mouth of God (Matt. 4:4), and God cannot and does not lie (Num. 23:19, John 17:17, Titus 1:2, Heb. 6:8, Ps. 119:160).

Charles Colson said:

"The Bible – banned, burned, beloved. More widely read, more frequently attacked than any other book in history. Generations of intellectuals have attempted to discredit it, dictators of every age have outlawed it and executed those who read it. Yet soldiers carry it into battle believing it more powerful than their weapons. Fragments of it smuggled into solitary prison cells have transformed ruthless killers into gentle saints."

Teddy Roosevelt said:

"A thorough knowledge of the Bible is more important than a college education."

Queen Elizabeth said:

"To what greater inspiration and counsel can we turn than to the imperishable truth to be found in this Treasure House, the Bible?"

The wisdom of the Bible is a wisdom that does not come from the world. It is supernatural in content and design. Its teachings are profitable for doctrine, for reproof, for correction and for instruction in righteousness (2 Tim. 3:16).

We are to hold dear the teachings of Jesus and do our best to follow them, for He is our Master and spiritual director, and knows all things. And we are to honor those who fear the Lord (Ps. 15:4).

"His divine power has given us everything we need for a godly life through our knowledge of Him who called us by His own glory and goodness. Through these He has given us His very great and precious promises, so that through them you may participate in the divine nature, having escaped the corruption in the world caused by evil desires." - 2 Pet. 1:3-4.

Actions Not Good Wishes

Most Christians are familiar with the importance of action versus good wishes, for it is taught throughout the Bible. For example, the parables exemplify action – people building houses, towers and foundations, sowing and reaping, spinning and weaving – and they stress the importance of utilizing the talents we were given and the skills we have learned to accomplish whatever needs to be done.

Jesus, Himself, was constantly active, always working towards accomplishing a goal or objective of His mission, hardly ever resting but continuously healing the sick, casting out evil spirits, cleansing lepers, giving sight to the blind and hearing to the deaf, raising the dead, forgiving sins and preaching the gospel. And when He was not working, He was praying. None of His days could have been fuller. He tells us by example that a man should be constructively occupied and constantly active, and praying whenever he can.

The duty falls on all Christians, and in particular teachers and ministers, to rightly divide the Word of truth (2 Tim. 2:15), but we are seeing more and more instances of where this duty has fallen by the wayside.

Remaining active becomes more difficult with age, but its benefits never cease. We cannot be lazy; we're not to give in to the pulls of leisure and forgetfulness no matter how strong such pulls may be. We should strive to improve our temporal and spiritual heath, for doing so ensures our effectiveness as ambassadors of Christ.

Idleness is said to be the parent of every sin, whereas labor favors virtue. "Let him labor working with his hands." (Eph. 4:8).

Christianity in a nutshell is this: he who is one in heart with God is a Christian, and he who trusts God loves Christ and strives to be as perfect by grace as He is by nature.

In giving the Great Commission (Matt. 28:19-20, Mark 16:15) to us, God says:

"Now therefore, go, and I will be with your mouth and teach you what you shall say." - Ex. 4:12.

Chapter 18 Parables

Some of the parables have been briefly cited in previous chapters, and the parable of the *Wheat and the Tares* was explained in the chapter on His Winnowing Fan. We now see them, and others, in more detail. They are extremely instructive and complement the previously discussed crucial but seldom preached messages and positions of our Lord, Jesus Christ.

The word "parable" is defined in the dictionary as a story told by Jesus to illustrate divine truths. They are interesting from many perspectives, for there is much more in them than what may be seen in the first reading. They are profound statements of simple truths that provide moral lessons for everyone.

The Parable of the Faithful Servant and the Evil Servant (Luke 12:35-40, and 45-48)

"Let your waist be girded and your lamps burning; and you yourselves be like men who wait for their master, when he will return from the wedding, that when he comes and knocks they may open to him immediately. Blessed are those servants whom the master, when he comes, will find watching. Assuredly, I say to you that he will gird himself and have them sit down to eat, and will come and serve them. And if he should come in the second watch, or come in the third watch, and find them so, blessed are those servants. But know this, that if the master of the house had known what hour the thief would come, he would have watched and not allowed his house to be broken into. Therefore you also be ready, for the Son of Man is coming at an hour you do not expect... But if that servant says in his heart, 'My master is delaying his coming,' and begins to beat the male and female servants, and to eat and drink and be drunk, the master of that servant will come on a day when he is not looking for him, and at an hour when he is not aware, and will cut him in two and appoint him his portion with the unbelievers. And that servant who knew his master's will, and did not prepare himself or do according to his will, shall be beaten with many stripes. But he who did not know, yet committed things deserving of stripes, shall be beaten with few."

The parable teaches first, that we should always be at work for God. It is how He accomplishes His main work in the world – through us. We are not to shirk from our duty but continue in it. It also teaches our need to be expectant of His return, for He is coming back to the earth in due time, and we are to watch out for it, lest He come and find us in prodigal ways, carousing with drunkards and gluttons, and count us unworthy of Him.

The Parable of the Wedding Feast (Matt. 22:1-14)

"Jesus answered and spoke to them again by parables and said: 'The kingdom of heaven is like a certain king who arranged a marriage for his son, and sent out his servants to call those who were invited to the wedding; and they were not willing to come. Again, he sent out other servants, saying, 'Tell those who are invited, "See, I have prepared my dinner; my oxen and fatted cattle are killed, and all things are ready. Come to the wedding." But they made light of it and went their ways, one to his own farm, another to his business. And the rest seized his servants, treated them spitefully, and killed them. But when the king heard about it, he was furious. And he sent out his armies, destroyed those murderers, and burned up their city. Then he said to his servants, 'The wedding is ready, but those who were invited were not worthy. Therefore go into the highways, and as many as you find, invite to the wedding.' So those servants went out into the highways and gathered together all whom they found, both bad and good. And the wedding hall was filled with guests."

"But when the king came in to see the guests, he saw a man there who did not have on a wedding garment. So he said to him, 'Friend, how did you come in here without a wedding garment?' And he was speechless. Then the king said to the servants, 'Bind him hand and foot, take him away, and cast him into outer darkness; there will be weeping and gnashing of teeth.' For many are called, but few are chosen."

The invitation to come to the feast is sent to everyone, but you have to come on the king's terms. The meaning of the parable is similar to that of Jesus's message of division – we either conform to His ways or we will be forever doomed. The enemies of God will try to attend, but they will be shut out. The wedding garment signifies Jesus, those who are His. You have to be presentable to the king to be acceptable to Him.

Regarding the king sending out his armies to destroy those murderers and burning up their city, when the children of Israel were driven out of Egypt after God performed His ten miracles (Exodus Chapters 7-12), the Bible refers to them as the armies of God. They later destroyed most of the pagans who lived in the promised land.

The Parable of the Talents (Matt. 25:14-30)

"For the kingdom of heaven is like a man traveling to a far country, who called his own servants and delivered his goods to them. And to one he gave five talents, to another two, and to another one, to each according to his own ability; and immediately he went on a journey. Then he who had received the five talents went and traded with them, and made another five talents. And likewise he who had received two gained two more also. But he who had received one went and dug in the ground, and hid his lord's money. After a long time, the lord of those servants came and settled accounts with them.

"So he who had received five talents came and brought five other talents, saying, 'Lord, you delivered to me five talents; look, I have gained five more talents besides them.' His lord said to him, 'Well done, good and faithful servant; you were faithful over a few things, I will make you ruler over many things. Enter into the joy of your lord.' He also who had received two talents came and said, 'Lord, you delivered to me two talents; look, I have gained two more talents besides them.' His lord said to him, 'Well done, good and faithful servant; you have been faithful over a few things, I will make you ruler over many things. Enter into the joy of your lord.' "Then he who had received the one talent came and said, 'Lord, I knew you to be a hard man, reaping where you have not sown, and gathering where you have not scattered seed. And I was afraid, and went and hid your talent in the ground. Look, there you have what is yours.'

"But his lord answered and said to him, 'You wicked and lazy servant, you knew that I reap where I have not sown, and gather where I have not scattered seed. So you ought to have deposited my money with the bankers, and at my coming I would have received back my own with interest. So take the talent from him, and give it to him who has ten talents.

"For to everyone who has, more will be given, and he will have abundance; but from him who does not have, even what he has will be taken away. And cast the unprofitable servant into the outer darkness. There will be weeping and gnashing of teeth."

God is telling us in this passage that we must do with what have been given, and do it in profitable ways. Otherwise, it will be taken away from us and given to another who is more worthy to receive it.

The Parable of the Rich Fool (Luke 12:16-21)

"Then He spoke a parable to them, saying: "The ground of a certain rich man yielded plentifully. And he thought within himself, saying, 'What shall I do, since I have no room to store my crops?' So he said, 'I will do this: I will pull down my barns and build greater, and there I will store all my crops and my goods. And I will say to my soul, "Soul, you have many goods laid up for many years; take your ease; eat, drink, and be merry." But God said to him, 'Fool! This night your soul will be required of you; then whose will those things be which you have provided?' "So is he who lays up treasure for himself, and is not rich toward God."

The Parable of the Wise and Foolish Virgins (Matthew 25:1-13)

"Then the kingdom of heaven shall be likened to ten virgins who took their lamps and went out to meet the bridegroom. Now five of them were wise, and five were foolish. Those who were foolish took their lamps and took no oil with them, but the wise took oil in their vessels with their lamps. But while the bridegroom was delayed, they all slumbered and slept.

"And at midnight a cry was heard: 'Behold, the bridegroom is coming; go out to meet him!' Then all those virgins arose and trimmed their lamps. And the foolish said to the wise, 'Give us some of your oil, for our lamps are going out.' But the wise answered, saying, 'No, lest there should not be enough for us and you; but go rather to those who sell, and buy for yourselves.' And while they went to buy, the bridegroom came, and those who were ready went in with him to the wedding; and the door was shut. Afterward the other virgins came also, saying, 'Lord, Lord, open to us!' But he answered and said, 'Assuredly, I say to you, I do not know you. Watch therefore, for you know neither the day nor the hour in which the Son of Man is coming."

Not only does this parable teach the importance of resource- fulness, vigilance and preparedness, but it tells us who the bridegroom is, Jesus. The Lord announced in the Gospel of Mark that He is the bridegroom and His followers are the children of the bridegroom. It is from this and similar passages of Scripture that the Church contends that the body of Christ is the bride.

The above four parables, the parable of the *Faithful Servant and the Evil Servant*, the parable of the *Talents*, the parable of the *Rich Fool*, and the parable of the *Wise and Foolish Virgins*, clarify by analogy what God expects our conduct on earth to be. Does it mean that we can we never really retire, sit on our laurels and take it easy? It certainly seems to indicate it, for God wants us be achievers. Other parables that give this impression are presented below.

The Parable of the Ten Minas (Luke 19:24-27)

"Now as they heard these things, He spoke another parable, because He was near Jerusalem and because they thought the kingdom of God would appear immediately. Therefore He said: "A certain nobleman went into a far country to receive for himself a kingdom and to return. So he called ten of his servants, delivered to them ten minas, and said to them, 'Do business till I come.' But his citizens hated him, and sent a delegation after him, saying, 'We will not have this man to reign over us.' And so it was that when he returned, having received the kingdom, he then commanded these servants, to whom he had given the money, to be called to him, that he might know how much every man had gained by trading. Then came the first, saying, 'Master, your mina has earned ten minas.' And he said to him, 'Well done, good servant; because you were faithful in a very little, have authority over ten cities.' And the second came, saying, 'Master, your mina has earned five minas.' Likewise he said to him, 'You also be over five cities.'

"Then another came, saying, 'Master, here is your mina, which I have kept put away in a handkerchief. For I feared you, because you are an austere man. You collect what you did not deposit, and reap what you did not sow.' And he said to him, 'Out of your own mouth I will judge you, you wicked servant. You knew that I was an austere man, collecting what I did not deposit and reaping what I did not sow. Why then did you not put my money in the bank, that at my coming I might have collected it with interest?' "And he said to those who stood by, 'Take the mina from him, and give it to him who has ten minas.' (But they said to him, 'Master, he has ten minas.') 'For I say to you, that to everyone who has will be given; and from him who does not have, even what he has will be taken away from him. But bring here those enemies of mine, who did not want me to reign over them, and slay them before me.'"

The parable is similar to the Parable of the *Talents,* but with important differences. It was given to the people when Jesus corrected them about their belief that the kingdom of God would immediately come. As mentioned previously, the parable testifies that God is a great King, one who is fair to those He favors by giving them resources in which to steward, but who executes severe punishment on His enemies.

The Parable of the Importance of Watching (Mark 13:33-36)

208

"Take heed, watch and pray; for you do not know when the time is. It is like a man going to a far country, who left his house and gave authority to his servants, and to each his work, and commanded the doorkeeper to watch. Watch therefore, for you do not know when the master of the house is coming – in the evening, at midnight, at the crowing of the rooster, or in the morning – lest, coming suddenly, he find you sleeping."

We are to wait for Christ's imminent return.

The Parable of the Importance of Being Prepared (Luke 14:28-32)

"For which of you, intending to build a tower, does not sit down first and count the cost, whether he has enough to finish it– lest, after he has laid the foundation, and is not able to finish, all who see it begin to mock him, saying, 'This man began to build and was not able to finish'? Or what king, going to make war against another king, does not sit down first and consider whether he is able with ten thousand to meet him who comes against him with twenty thousand? Or else, while the other is still a great way off, he sends a delegation and asks conditions of peace."

It is folly to start a work before counting the costs and judging whether by our own strength we are capable of finishing it.

The Bible contains many passages that stress the importance, and the advantages, of hard work, and the imprudence of indolence or idleness. They include:

"Take a lesson from the ants, you lazybones. Learn from their ways and become wise! Though they have no prince or governor or ruler to make them work, they labor hard all summer, gathering food for the winter." - Prov. 6:6-8.

"Those too lazy to plow in the right season will have no food at the harvest." - Prov. 20:4.

"No one, having put his hand to the plow, and looking back, is fit for the kingdom of God." - Luke 9:62.

Ministers of Christ sometimes find themselves in Jerimiah's position of not wanting to preach, but being compelled to do so. Although it is easy to confuse an obsession with a compulsion, it could be that one comes from a craving to satisfy a desire and the other something that we would just rather not do at the time.

I believe that God has a way of working in each individual's life to bring out what He intended to be accomplished through them from the foundation of the world. If you feel unmistakably compelled to pursue something, it could be because of His will and influence in your life. If unsure, ask, and you will receive an answer (Luke 11:9-10).

The Parable of a Tree is Known by Its Fruit (Luke 6:43-45)

This parable is given multiple times in one form or other in the New Testament.

"For a good tree does not bear bad fruit, nor does a bad tree bear good fruit. For every tree is known by its own fruit. For men do not gather figs from thorns, nor do they gather grapes from a bramble bush. A good man out of the good treasure of his heart brings forth good; and an evil man out of the evil treasure of his heart brings forth evil. For out of the abundance of the heart his mouth speaks."

Matthew 7:15-20 is similar, but it has: "Every tree that does not bear good fruit is cut down and thrown into the fire." Matt. 3:10 and Luke 3:9 tell us that John the Baptist said much the same thing:

"Indeed the axe is already laid at the root of the trees; so every tree that does not bear good fruit is cut down and thrown into the fire." - Luke 3:9.

The parable is loaded with meaning. As discussed in the chapter on His Winnowing Fan, it portends the impending great Judgment. Also, like the other parables, it is meant to be instructive. It reveals an important fact about all of us – that we act and speak out of the good or evil treasures of our hearts.

"As a man thinketh in his heart, so is he." - Prov. 23:7.

The parable informs us that character is consistent with conduct. it tells us how to distinguish the just from the unjust, the good from the evil, and severely warns of the necessity of bearing good fruit.

It is important that we can, at least in most cases, discern character through a person's actions. But it's not as easy as one might think.

People have become experts at hiding their true natures (feelings), their true selves – the "real you" – from the world. Our culture teaches that we can be whatever we set our minds on being, and that the best way to be successful is to act like you're already there because then, they say, success will naturally follow. It is widely proclaimed in the media, especially in the cinema and television.

Every day we see the "self" pushed for profit in self-help books, magazines and webinars. We learn that the most important thing about a person is their outward appearance, how they appear or seem to be in the eyes of others. A person's character is not widely considered to be important. Truth and honesty are rated lower today than a person's outward appearance and impression they make on others. But God sees us the way we really are.

"The Lord sees not as man sees: man looks on the outward appearance, but the Lord looks on the heart." - 1 Sam, 16-7.

Many people join churches to fulfil a need for belonging and acceptance. They sing the songs and give mental assent to the doctrines, but they're not genuine followers of Jesus unless there has been a transformation in their lives. They take communion (the Eucharist) commemorating the Lord death, but are like dangerous reefs that shipwreck (Jude 1:12), and clouds without rain, boasting of gifts they have never given (Prov. 25:14).

An increasing number are going out from the body of Christ but were never really part of it. They are apostates, as discussed in 1 John 2:19, once professing the religion of the Savior but never really belonging to the church of Christ. Instead of being servants of God, they are servants of the devil, and turn out to be hypocrites or heretics, to the scandal of the church. They are deceivers who apostatize the inspired Word of God and preach a Jesus other than the Jesus of the Bible. These things, and more, occur so that their real character might be developed (1 John 2:19).

They are false apostles, deceitful workers, transforming themselves into apostles of Christ, but having the spirit and motivation of the father of lies (2 Cor. 11:13-14). The Lord will punish them by blindness – scriptural blindness – and in the end eternal damnation.

"Whoever has sinned against Me, I will blot out of My book." - Ex. 32:33.

The good fruit accepts the Son and the Father, but the bad fruit acknowledges neither. Whoever rejects the Son, rejects the Father also (Luke 10:16, 1 John 2:23) and brings the wrath of God upon themselves (Matt. 10:33, John 3:36).

When Jesus went to the fig tree and found no fruit, He cursed it and it withered away and died (Mark 11:12-21). Let the withered fig tree be a lesson to us all. We are unfruitful and wither away when we turn our backs on God and His Word.

Summary

The most significant aspect about the parables is their effect on us. They grab us on a personal level. They make us pause for reflection. How am I doing? What kind of success am I having in bearing good fruit? Am I being cultivated day by day by spending time in God's Word and in prayer? Is my inner self being transformed in the ways that Jesus talked about?

Chapter 19 The Importance of a Worldview

"Even the most casual survey of the world around us – a world torn by anxieties and self-doubt, by depression and despair, by confrontation and alienation, by violence committed in the name of peace – males it painfully obvious that our enormous technological prowess has brought no clear and certain answers to the most basic and important needs of man's mind and soul." - Alfred Armand Montapert.

There are many theories that are premised on faulty reasoning and supposition. The theory of evolution, the leading philosophy of the world, influences how millions of people view the origin and evolution of the animal kingdom, including man. There is also the universal perception that the earth is round and not flat, which is not, however, what commonsense, logic and the Bible indicate it is.

As discussed previously, our world is considered by almost everyone to be round in shape, spinning on its axis and orbiting the Sun, one of many habitable planets in an ever-expanding universe, traveling on an endless and purposeless journey through space. It is the worldview which has prevailed for hundreds of years – the great spinning ball earth worldview. What does this tell us? Either that most people believe popular opinion over the Bible, or that they are ignorant of the Word of God and prefer to ignore commonsense and logic. But those who know the Bible and are well acquainted with it have serious doubts about what modern science claims is the true nature of the world, and many struggle with the discrepancies.

The global earth theory has been drilled into each of us to such an extent that it has literally become a part of our lives. However, neither the theory of heliocentrism nor the theory of evolution, which is a spin-off of the global earth theory, has ever been proved. What many scientists claim as infallible proofs are riddled with contradictions, incongruities and inconsistencies. Instead of being rooted in truth, both theories are premised on faulty reasoning and suppositions.

But God wouldn't want it that way. He would want everyone to see the world as it really is because He made it expressly for us, not only to learn about and benefit from, but to enjoy, not to be visited by aliens from outer space, or for us to someday leave and find a neighboring world to migrate to, but so that every person in every generation would, by their own abilities and skills, come to sufficiently understand and appreciate the great wonder of the creation, and that this would, hopefully, lead people to make proper use of it.

Add to these things the overworked and underpaid status of most of the souls now living on earth, and you almost have the complete picture of how things are in the 21st century.

Our worldview plays a major role in how we consider and interpret the world around us. Think not? Then ask yourself how differently things would look to you, including the Sun and Moon, and how differently you would see yourself fitting in with the overall scheme of things, if you knew for sure that the earth was not round and moving, but flat and motionless.

How we view the world and our place in it affects every aspect of our lives, because thoughts control our reality. Worldview affects not only how we view ourselves, our friends, our loved ones, but politics, sports, our jobs, our outlook on life and even the stock market – practically everything about our lives. It has the power to alter perceptions, direct motives and shape events.

Worldview affects how we address the basic questions of life: Where did we come from? Why are we here? Is there right and wrong? What happens when we die?

The global earth theory has given birth to the widespread belief that the universe is infinite and that the earth and solar system are but specks of dust lost in the vastness of space. It has spawned the belief that intelligent life exists on other worlds outside the solar system, which is called the doctrine of the plurality of worlds, a belief that is fostered by our educational system, the media and most of the religions of the world.

The global earth theory and the theory of evolution became a part of most people's lives in grade or elementary school, when they were initially instilled in us by our teachers. We are easily influenced by what others think.

Public opinion is a powerful force, and can become the controlling force in our lives. Some of us are prisoners of public opinion, not thinking for ourselves.

We are a frightened people, excessively worried about what others think, whether it is about us or about things in general, and how we should live in ways that would make others like us more. While most people are concerned about the purpose and meaning of life (or, as some may wonder, whether there is purpose and meaning to life), we are inclined to believe what others tell us is true, and how we conform to popular opinion determines to a large extent who we are. It explains why many believe in evolution and a round earth.

"The deep need to be accepted and the fear of being rejected are powerful forces. They form an unconscious conspiracy that makes us believe we want what we don't want and feel what we don't feel. The more we become assimilated into "The World," the more we become a stranger to ourselves, even to the extent that we are not sure why we enjoy something."[87]

Atheism, which is fostered by the belief in evolution and a global earth, creates irreconcilable differences with the teachings of the Bible, teachings that clearly tell us that we were created for a reason, and that each of us is endowed with a spirit, or soul, which is the exclusive property of God, and that it is He to whom we must present ourselves for judgement in the end.

Atheists and many others today believe that there are no moral standards, but that right and wrong are relative terms that depend on the individual and/or the circumstances involved. They are given over to believing that whatever is pleasing is right for them to do. If you feel like committing a crime, then just "Do you" and commit it.

When Jesus walked the earth, He told the crowds that He did not come to abolish the Law or the Prophets, but to fulfill them and their teachings. The standards of morality given to mankind in the law of Moses, including the Ten Commandments, are important, for they have relevance for mankind and significance in the eyes of God. Jesus said that unless your righteousness exceeds the righteousness of the scribes and Pharisees, you will by no means enter into the kingdom of heaven.

The Bible is our standard for truth. Without its moral standards, human rights, including the rights of the unborn innocent, become provisional and entirely dependent on political dogma or popular opinion.

---

[87] Mark Foley, The Dark Night.

In the creation account, God divided the light from the darkness, and He still does. He draws the lines. How can we know what is right and wrong? God tells us what is right and wrong. He gives us His ordinances, His precepts and His principles. There is just as much difference between right and wrong as there is between light and darkness.

Sir Isaac Newton said,

"Atheism is so senseless. When I look at the solar system, I see the earth at the right distance from the Sun to receive the proper amounts of heat and light. This did not happen by chance."[88]

Having an incorrect or misleading worldview causes inner tension and anxiety. It leads to despondency and confusion, giving rise to a nagging suspicion that something is not quite right.

We are witnessing many things today that are wrong with the world. A dysphoria, or a general feeling of dissatisfaction with life, has descended upon millions of the earth's inhabitants. Injustice and intolerance abound, and feelings of bitterness, anger, resentment, confusion and hopelessness are everywhere. Disillusionment, negativity and suffering are the common lot of people throughout the world. While worldview cannot be blamed for all the bad that happens to people, it can certainly be said to be a big contributor.

A worldview that goes against reason and intuition creates subtle but harmful effects on mind and body, such as prevailing undercurrents of vexation, or a feeling that something isn't quite right, and so tension builds.

---

[88] https:/www.azquotes.com/quote/799978.

When I think of the possibility of being on an insignificant speck of driftwood drifting aimlessly in the vast ocean of outer space, I feel dispirited and piteous. What a way to go through a single day, not to mention an entire lifetime!

The dignity with which man was endowed at the creation has been lost on the world. Global earth science has taken it away, because it denies the existence of God and rejects the Bible, considering it antiquated and having little or no relevance to today's world.

The global earth theory has brought about a general ignorance of the Word of God. The Bible is being shunned by men, women and children for no other reason than the widespread belief, strengthened daily by the media, that we live on a spiritless globe.

However, the Bible is not only applicable, but essential, for solving the problems of today, including the many problems we now face in our society. Its word is sharper than a two-edged sword, and cuts right to the core of man's condition. It has saved millions from being physically and spiritually wrecked by the many pitfalls and tragedies that are common to life, and has helped millions more who needed strength and hope in time of need.

The prevalent worldview reminds me of the frog-in-the-pot story. If you put a frog in a pot of boiling water, the frog will immediately jump out, but if you put it in a pot of room temperature water and then slowly bring it to a boil, it will stay in the pot until it dies.

More people are opting out of marriage and family life than ever before. They're purposely alienating themselves from others, including members of the opposite sex. One of the results of this distancing is the declining birth rate.[89] Another is that childcare is placed in the hands of complete strangers, many of whom are not qualified for the task, which does not portend well for the future generations. Preventing and reversing these trends can only occur if reigning attitudes about life are changed.

Wernher von Braun said,

"Science does not have a moral dimension."[90]

The way we see ourselves matters. It affects how we live. It affects how we treat others. It affects the quality of life for each and all of us. Without moral grounding, without concern for how our thoughts and actions affect others, not even democracy is capable of ensuring peaceful stability in the world.

However, when we turn to the Bible and acknowledge our need for guidance and wisdom, we find consolation in times of grief, help in times of need and contentment in times of anger, frustration and hopelessness.

When we focus our attention on God, a profound peace descends upon us. It leads not only to the momentary relief of stress and worry, but to improved mental health and emotional stability. It relieves us of the oppressive urgency of the present, the regret of the past, and the fear of the future.

Thomas Paine said,

"The two beliefs – modern astronomy and the Bible – cannot be

---

[89] According to CDC statistics, the U.S. birth rate is currently 16 percent below the amount needed to replace our population over time. Source: https://www.cnn.com/2019/01/10/health/us-fertility-rate-replacement-cdc-study.
[90] https://www.azquotes.com/author/1841-Wernher_von_Braun.

held together in the same mind. He who thinks he believes both has thought very little of either."[91]

Many websites claim that the soul does not exist, that death is the end of existence and that an afterlife is only a figment of someone's imagination. However, as mentioned previously, the Bible tells us that when a person dies, the soul, which is one's true self, ends up in one of two places, a place of malevolent torment, confusion and darkness, or a place of benevolent peace, joy and enlightenment. Many people blame God for the seemingly unfair practice of eternally damning people for their sins because they are not able to see that there are absolutes in afterlife as there are absolutes in life.

In the world there are love and hate, right and wrong, hot and cold, light and darkness, good and evil, truth and falsehood, the sacred and the profane. Likewise, there is a heaven and a hell. But only one awaits each of us. The decisions made in life determine the soul's eternal destination.

A worldview that denies the existence of the soul discounts a crucial part of a person's reality.

We all have a natural desire to live forever. It can only have originated from our having a beginning in the mind of God, the Eternal One. It is why we are never completely at home with a worldview that denies or excludes the Creator, for such a worldview is intuitively wrong.

How did the prevalent worldview come about?

It was in the 16th and 17th centuries that worldview changed

---

[91] Thomas Winship, Zetetic Cosmogony,

fundamentally based on the theories of Copernicus (1473-1543), Galileo (1564-1647) and Newton (1642-1727). It was the time of the Scientific Revolution when science moved to the forefront of social and economic thinking, and it altered man's views on practically everything. It was a time in which new developments took place in the physical sciences, such as physics, chemistry and astronomy, developments that caused man to think differently about the world. It created a gulf between the Bible and science.

The gulf was broadened by what is called the Age of Enlightenment, a time when philosophers like René Descartes (1596-1650) and Immanuel Kant (1724-1804) proceeded to the stage, bringing with them new ideas about who man was.

"Cogito, ergo sum." ("I think, therefore I am.") - René Descartes.

The resulting framework of thought, which persists to this day, enthrones both man and science, and dethrones God. It lifts man into a temporary heady sense of being his own god, of knowing all things, of being right, while the purpose of the Gospel is to convict him of being altogether wrong.

Job, the most perfect man in God's sight except for our Lord, Himself, said, "I am vile."

"A man may feel great and important while he stands in in own garden, but let him stand beneath the stupendous heights of snow-capped peaks, let him be in the mighty ocean when its waves run mountain-high, and then he will see himself to be the puny pigmy he really is, then only will he realize his own impotence, and thankfully cast himself on God's omnipotence." - E. W. Bullinger.

No more was man considered to be a creature who came from God, and who may come to know God. No more was he endowed with his birthright dignity. Instead, he became a product of mere chance, having no God to whom he is accountable. It is a framework of thought that puts man at the center of his own universe.

"Now entering my own universe, pop 1." - Road sign in a magazine advertisement.

Historians consider Descartes and Kant primarily responsible for the man-centered (humanistic) worldview that caused, among other things, the tragic French Revolution, which Charles Dickens, in *A Tale of Two Cities*, called "the leprosy of unreality." Both philosophers are considered fathers of what is called "modern rationalism," a philosophy claiming that man is only what he believes he is, rather than what the Bible says he is.

This heliocentric worldview greatly contributed to the rise of the atheistic and materialistic philosophies of the late 19th century that were inspired by German, English and Russian thinkers, such as Hegel, Nietzsche, Chamberlain, Marx and Lenin, whose strong opinions about man, society and religion were greatly responsible for the Russian Revolution and the Second World War that followed, and for the terrible loss of life, including the atrocities and genocides that took place during those upheavals.

If we believe that everything is relative, then many wrongful acts are condoned, including the intentional killing of innocent human beings, those who are either unwanted or unneeded, such as the unfortunate victims of genetic disorders, the aged, the infirm and fetuses, beings who are blessed with life but who are considered expendable for personal or economic reasons, or for no reason at all.

It makes murder an expediency rather than a sin. It disregards the rights of others, and the express purpose that God intended for every living soul – to know Him and have fellowship with Him.

"You shall not curse the deaf, nor put a stumbling block before the blind, but shall fear your God. I am the Lord." - Lev. 19:14.

"The Lord said to him, "Who makes the mute, the deaf, the seeing, or the blind? Have not I, the Lord?" - Ex. 4:11.

Without the moral teachings of the Bible, including its forewarning that everyone will be judged for their actions and words (Matt. 25: 31-46), we become our own rule makers, which leads to becoming our own judges and disowning God. If no one has a soul, or spirit, then it can be believed that we are no more than what we think we are.

John Adams said,

"The preservation of liberty depends upon the intellectual and moral character of the people. As long as knowledge and virtue are diffused among the body of a nation, it is impossible that they should be enslaved."[92]

It may be said that the theory of a global earth has brought upon this world more misery, confusion and suffering than perhaps anything else.

Any nation, state, province, philosophy, religion, political party or worldview that does not respect the lives of others does not respect liberty or God.

---

[92] David McCullough, John Adams.

224

Pope John Paul II, who reigned as Pope from 1978 until his death in 2005, said of age of rationalism:

"The consequence was that man was supposed to live by his reason alone, as if God did not exist. Not only was it necessary to leave God out of the objective knowledge of the world, since the existence of a Creator or of Providence was in no way helpful to science, it was also necessary to act as if God did not exist, as if God were not interested in the world. The rationalism of the Enlightenment was able to accept a God outside of the world primarily because it was an unverifiable hypothesis. It was crucial, however, that such a God be expelled from the world."[93]

A shift in thought had taken place from the belief that man's immortal soul had significance in the eyes of God, and therefore should have significance in the eyes of men, to a science-centered, self-centered, atheistic worldview (which persists today) that holds that man is merely an accident of Nature, whose sole purpose for existence is to satisfy himself with the material things of this world.

"If there is no God, and everyone is just an accident, then all that really matters is me, me, me. They have turned Madonna, the Mother of God, into a material girl living in a material world."[94]

Woodrow Wilson said,

"It is only once in a generation that a people can be lifted above material things."

By putting material things in the forefront of our lives, many of us

---

[93] Pope John Paul II n his 1994 book, Crossing the Threshold of Hope.
[94] Eric Dubay, 200 Proofs Earth is Not a Spinning Ball.

have neglected the weightier matters of life, such as family, health and well-being, acts of compassion and charity, inner peace, and our relationship to the Creator.

After Russian cosmonaut Yuri Gagarin returned to earth from his historic first orbital spaceflight in 1961, he announced,

"I looked and looked and looked, but I didn't see God."[95]

Then, in 1962, Andriyan Nikolayev, on returning to earth from his Vostok III spaceflight, said, "I didn't see God up there."[96]

Both messages echo the global earth atheistic worldview, which is a core belief of all communist nations. It has been a fundamental part of Soviet and Communist China dogma, or ideology, since Lenin. It holds that God exists only in one's imagination, and that religion is the opium (narcotic addiction) of the masses. It has been responsible for the imprisonment and torture of countless human beings, which continues to this day in Communist China.

"For the time will come when people will not put up with sound doctrine. Instead, to suit their own desires, they will gather around them a great number of teachers to say what their itching ears want to hear. They will turn their ears away from the truth and turn aside to myths." - 2 Tim. 4:3-4.

Ronald Reagan, the then future 40th President of the United States, used both statements of the cosmonauts to emphasize what he widely proclaimed in the 1950s about Soviet Russia, that it was "Godless Communism."[97] [98]

---

[95] Paul Kengor, God and Ronald Reagan.
[96] Ibid.
[97] Ibid.

As astronaut Gordon Cooper states in his book, *Leap of Faith*,

"If the cosmonauts had not known God here on earth, they were not going to find Him a hundred and fifty miles above the earth."

"Professing to be wise, they became fools." - Rom. 1:22.

The concept of the world being an incidental result of some cosmic accident is contrary to logic and common sense, because He who made us in His likeness is a God of Reason.

Do you really believe that God would select an insignificant world, one of billions of accidentally formed planets whirling aimlessly through a cold, lifeless and endless void, upon which to descend and assume human form? Our world must be very, very special, indeed, for the Son of God to have dwelt among us.

Somehow, everyone knows that going nowhere from nowhere is wrong and pointless, and that we were meant for better things.

"I will destroy the wisdom of the wise, and bring to nothing the understanding of the prudent. Where is the wise? Where is the scribe? Where is the disputer of this age? Has not God made foolish the wisdom of this world?" - 1 Cor. 1:19 -20.

Thomas Winship said,

"Nature and the Bible are in perfect agreement."

The most important question that one can ask is "Why?" If we

---

[98] According to Stalin's daughter who was present at Stalin's death, right before Stalin died, he suddenly became conscious, opened his eyes wide, raised himself up from his bed and shook his fist in rage at God. Then he fell back and died.

postpone asking it until the end of our lives, the grave danger exists of losing much more than our wealth or position in the world. Speculation and theory cannot satisfy us. St. Augustine of Hippo said, "You have made us for Yourself, O Lord, and our hearts are restless until they rest in You."

The worldview we carry with us daily not only affects our thoughts and actions but defines the rest of our lives. It determines our perceptions of interconnectedness, our place in the integral web of things, and how we perceive God.

The truths of the Bible have been the basis for the most significant of human developments, including democratic government, the laws of the land, equal pay for equal work, the criminal justice system and the Universal Declaration of Human Rights. It has been the reason behind the abolition of child labor, the abolition of slavery, women's suffrage and the battle against abortion.

A proper worldview may not work magic on many of life's struggles and misfortunes, but it does wonders for mental health and well-being because it fosters mental clarity, a clarity that disperses the mental haze that most people carry with them and consider to be perfectly normal. When we begin questioning the validity of the global earth theory and adopt a worldview that is in line with the teachings of the Bible, mental clarity descends upon us.

The Bible teaches that this world is the only world there is. It never suggests or alludes to any other possibility. It never even hints that there could be life on other worlds. Such ideas are the inventions of unbridled thoughts and imaginations that are consistent with the teachings of modern science, but not with God's Word.

Instead of being formed by chance for no particular reason, the Bible tells us that the world came into existence for a purpose, which was for humankind to subdue, populate and make the best possible use of, not only for its survival, but for its physical and spiritual development, so that one day, hopefully of its own volition, it would come to know its Creator.

As mentioned previously, the Bible describes the earth using words such as:

"Thus says God the Lord, who created the heavens and stretched them out, who spread forth the earth and that which comes from it, who gives breath to the people on it, and spirit to those who walk on it." - Isa. 42:5.

He stretched out the heavens and spread forth the earth. He spread it forth, or spread it out, as one would spread peanut butter on a slice of bread. He didn't make it into a ball and start it spinning. He spread the earth out.

The Bible tells us that the Sun, Moon and heavens move over the earth, just as they are observed to do. It describes a firmament in which the heavenly objects are placed. It describes man as having central, not incidental, importance to the world. As discussed in the chapter on Heaven, the Bible teaches that there is nothing outside or above the firmament except for the upper waters and Heaven, which is God's abode, and that all the world or universe as we know it is contained beneath the firmament, all that we can know and see, including the Sun, Moon, planets, stars and heavenly objects.

Moreover, God has given Jesus all authority on earth and in Heaven (Matt. 28:18, John 5:26-29, Rev. 19:11-13), implying that these are the only two realms that exist, and that they contain everything we can know and see, including the stars, galaxies and planets. The Bible does not mention, or allude to, an expansive universe or the existence of other worlds that scientists tell us are separate from the earth and heaven. In not alluding to them, it seems to imply and even proclaim that they are not separate from the earth, but rather part of the realm that God gave Jesus to rule.

This is how the Bible describes the world. It is how the world should be viewed. It is the correct view, the view that is in harmony with the intellect and the intuition.

People say that our modern-day conception of the universe was unknown to the writers of Scripture, and, as such, Scripture cannot be trusted to give us the correct view of the world/universe/cosmos. It is true that the current, unproven theories of the Big Bang and the origin of the Sun, solar system and stars were unknown at the time the Old and New testaments were written, but it does not undermine the veracity of the Scriptures.

As discussed in the chapter on The Day the Sun and Moon Stood Still, and Other Miracles, ancient astronomers, such as the Babylonians, were experts at observing, predicting and cataloging the movements of the heavenly bodies. They spent much of their time out of doors, unlike modern astronomers who spend most of their time in offices and cubes monitoring computers that run the optical, radio, infrared, ultraviolet, X-ray and gamma ray telescopes and antennae that are used to investigate the universe. It is my belief that astronomers have long lost touch with the reality of the night sky.

Ancient astronomers had the sky in its full glory for their ceiling. The only lights they had at night, except for the luminaries in the sky, were fires and torches. By just stepping away from them for a few minutes their eyes could easily adjust to the dark. Because of their closeness to Nature, they were able to create very accurate models of the heavens using precision astronomical instruments made of brick and stone.[99]

Astronomy, unlike other sciences, does not allow for experiment-ation. The astronomer cannot change the conditions of space or what lies it. He cannot perform tests on celestial objects. He cannot add, remove, move around, or change in any way what is up in the sky. For example, he cannot tear stars or planets apart to see what is in them or what makes them tick. He can only observe them.

Early astronomers used the concept of the celestial sphere to explain the geocentric movement of the heavenly objects. Divided into halves by the celestial equator, a celestial sphere could be considered close to the earth, or infinite in radius. It was used to explain the difference in the observed motions of the heavenly objects, including the retrograde motion of the superior planets.[100] [101]

"The ancients assumed the literal truth of the stars being attached to a celestial sphere, revolving about the earth in one day, and a fixed earth. All objects in the sky may be conceived as being projected upon the inner surface of the celestial sphere…All celestial objects seem equally far away, as if fixed onto the inside of a sphere with a large but unknown radius, which appears to rotate westward overhead; meanwhile, earth underfoot seems to remain still…. Objects are seen as if projected onto a dome."[102]

---

[99] See, for example: https://www.afar.com/places/jantar-mantar-astronomical-observatory-jaipur.
[100] https://en.wikipedia.org/wiki/Celestial_sphere.
[101] https://en.wikipedia.org/wiki/Opposition_(planets).
[102] Ibid.

Star Distances

If we are to believe modern astronomers, many of the stars visible to the naked eye are trillions of miles away from the earth, although such distances are very difficult to measure. For example, Alpha Centauri, the nearest star, is said to be about 4.2 lightyears away, or 24.7 trillion miles from earth.[103]

"Distance is the most important and most difficult quantity to measure in astronomy."[104]

Astronomers also claim that the universe is populated by billions and billions of stars, and that when we look up at any star we are in effect looking backwards through time, and that the star we are viewing may no longer be there. For example, it could have exploded 500,000 years ago and we would not know it because its different light fingerprint would not have reached us yet.

However, assertions such as these present several difficulties. If space really contains so many stars, even if they are very distant from the earth, then why isn't the night sky full of stars and blinding with light?

Astronomers have offered various theories to explain this inconsistency, which is called "Olbers' Paradox." The most accepted theory is that the universe keeps expanding based on the Big Bang,[105] meaning that stars are constantly moving away from us, which causes their light to get dimmer with time.

---

[103] A lightyear is 5.88 trillion miles. Ref. www.brittanica.com › Demystified › Science.)

[104] https://www. astronomy.ohio-state.edu/~pogge/Ast162/Unit1/distances.html.

[105] A cataclysmic event that supposedly took place 13.8 billion years ago. Reference https://www.en.wikipedia.org › wiki › Big_Bang.

Even if this were true, however, the implications of Olbers' Paradox still hold. Everywhere we look in the night sky there should be some light. But what do we observe? Except for times of moonlight, almost total darkness. Although stars and constellations can be seen away from big cities when our eyes adjust to the dark, the night sky is darker than it should be if there are billions and billions of stars in the universe. Even when using binoculars or telescopes, we are never blinded by the light of the night sky.

In fact, scientists tell us that light coming from all the stars amounts to no more than a 60-Watt lightbulb shining 5.5 miles away.[106] A very faint lightshow indeed! We are once again confronted with incongruities and inconsistencies with modern science's own statements. It is apparent that something is wrong with modern astronomy's explanation for why the night sky is not full of light.

It is interesting to note that, according to Einstein's General Theory of Relativity, Olbers' Paradox is valid.[107]

The proof offered by modern astronomers for the stars receding from earth is what they call "redshift." Redshift is defined as the displacement of spectral lines in the light coming from distant stars and galaxies towards longer wavelengths (that is, the red end of the spectrum). It is said to be a Doppler-like effect which is proportional to the velocity of recession, and thus to the distance the stars and galaxies are assumed to be from the earth.[108]

---

[106] www.theatlantic.com/science/archive/2018/11/starlight-universe-blazar-galaxy/576934/.

[107] https://www.en.wikipedia.org › wiki › Olbers'_paradox.

[108] Fred Hoyle, Frontiers of Astronomy.

"When we pass starlight through a prism (or similar device suitable for telescopes, such as diffraction gratings), we see a forest of absorption lines from hydrogen, helium, sodium, and so on. However, if that star is hurtling away from us, all those absorption lines undergo a Doppler shift and move toward the red part of the rainbow. This is what we call a redshift. For stars heading toward us, the opposite happens, and the lines are shifted toward the blue end of the spectrum."[109]

The problem with this explanation, however, is how do we know from redshift that stars are moving away from us? We reach the conclusion only because we observe a shift in the absorption lines that are postulated to occur because the stars are moving away. But this is circular logic. It is a conclusion based on assuming the truth of what we are trying to prove.

"Circular reasoning (Latin: circulus in probando, "circle in proving"; also known as circular logic) is a logical fallacy in which the reasoner begins with what they are trying to end with.[110]

Since astronomy does not allow for experimentation, the astronomer cannot change the conditions of space, or what lies in it, to prove his theories. He can only try to understand the world/cosmos/universe from observation. The redshift theory is further refuted by the author in another book, which provides more scientific evidence of its tenuousness.

Astronomers also use the appearance of stars, galaxies and other celestial objects to determine their relative distances from the earth. For example, a smaller looking galaxy and one dimmer in brightness than others is assumed to be farther away from the

---

[109]www.earthsky.org › astronomy-essentials › what-is-a-redshift.
[110] www.en.wikipedia.org › wiki › Circular_reasoning.

234

earth.[111] But is that a valid assumption? It could be that the apparent size and/or brightness of galaxies has little or nothing to do with their distances from the earth. It could be that God made them larger and smaller and brighter and dimmer when He placed them in the firmament. Therefore, this fundamental assumption of astronomy appears to be mere conjecture.

"There is one glory of the Sun, another glory of the Moon, and another glory of the stars; for one star differs from another star in glory." - 1 Cor. 15:41.

While we're discussing galaxies, it should be mentioned that the Milky Way is assumed to be a spiral galaxy because spiral galaxies can be seen through telescopes. However, no one has actually observed the Milky Way from a sufficient distance to prove that it is a spiral galaxy, or a galaxy at all. It is another case of monkey see, monkey do, similar to astronomers telling us that the earth is a globe because the Sun, Moon and planets are observed to be globes.

As mentioned previously, the Bible says that someday the stars will fall to the earth.

"Immediately after the tribulation of those days the Sun will be darkened, and the Moon will not give its light, and the stars will fall from heaven, and the powers of the heavens will be shaken." - Matt. 24:29.

"And the stars will be falling from heaven, and the powers in the heavens will be shaken." - Mark 13:25.

---

[111] www.skyserver.sdss.org/dr1/en/proj/basic/universe/distances.

"And the stars of the sky fell to the earth as the fig tree sheds its winter fruit when shaken by a gale." - Rev. 6:13.

These verses, and also Isaiah 34:4, affirm that the stars are placed in the firmament. However, modern astronomers deny these things.

As for new stars, we should be able to see them blooming into sight as time goes by, if what astronomers say is true, because their light would eventually reach the earth from their multi-lightyear distances away. But we never see new stars blinking on. The stars that we observe are the same stars that have always been seen in the sky. Ever since astronomers first began cataloging the stars, no stars have ever been seen to disappear and no new stars have ever popped into view. Some have gone supernova, but the stars the Babylonians observed thousands of years ago are basically the same stars observed today. No stars have ever vanished from the sky, as they would have if they were actually receding from us, and no new stars have ever been observed with the naked eye. However, both would be common occurrences, if not during a particular lifetime then certainly over hundreds of years, if what astronomers are saying is true.

Of course, astronomers have discovered "new" stars using optical, infrared and other telescopes, but it is only because of the ability of these instruments to detect what is not visible to the naked eye that such things have been discovered, and for this reason they are not really new stars at all, but stars that have always existed.

As stated in the chapter on What the Bible Says is the Configuration of the World, I have studied, researched and observed the many incongruities and inconsistencies that exist in the explanations that modern science has for the nature of the world, which has been indoctrinated into most of us since birth –

that the earth is a spinning ball hurtling through space around the Sun. It is my belief that apart from the divinely inspired Word of God, no theory, no matter how simple or complex it may be, including the theory of the Big Bang, the theory of the origin of the solar system, the theory of evolution, and the global earth theory, can adequately explain the true nature of the world.

The Lord's prayer (Matt. 6:5-15) reads, "Our Father, who is in heaven, hallowed by Your name. Your kingdom come and your will be done on earth as it is in heaven..." It, too, implies that all things that we are able to observe are contained either on earth or in heaven. It doesn't mention or allude to the vast universe of stars or other worlds that we commonly hear about.

Would the Lord ever die on the cross for the sins of the world if our world was only one of many, many worlds? It would mean He would have to die again and again on each of those worlds as well. But Scripture tells us that He died once and for all (Rom. 6:10), and that Scripture cannot be broken (John 10:35), meaning that it is indestructible and will always stand. Numbers 23:19 states, "Has He said, and will He not do? Or has He spoken, and will He not make it good?"

If we adhered to the Bible instead of popular opinion, it would raise our consciousness, since we intuitively know that God created the world and that it was not formed in any other way.

"When the consciousness of one person is raised, the whole of humanity is raised." - M. Basil Pennington, O.C.S.O.

Our hope, our reliance should not be in science or man or public opinion. Rather, our focus should be on the Creator, and this important principle is taught throughout the Bible.

"It is better to take refuge in the Lord than to trust in man." - Ps. 118:8.

"Stop regarding man in whose nostrils is breath, for of what account is he?" - Isa. 2:22.

"Behold, they have rejected the word of the Lord; so what wisdom do they have?" - Jer. 8:9.

"For am I now seeking the approval of man, or of God? Or am I trying to please man? If I were still trying to please man, I would not be a servant of Christ." - Gal. 1:10.

The right worldview does not limit us, it liberates us, for we are never more at ease or in a better frame of mind than when we realize the truth about ourselves and why we are here. How encouraging it would be if we believed in the right worldview as we awaken to each new day!

Chapter 20 War and Peace

In this chapter, we see various viewpoints on whether it is right for Christians to participate in war. Several subjects are taken up. Is it right to fight against the enemies of Christ, or to abstain from fighting? Are there any precedents in the Bible for what direction should be taken? Does God support war?

These are questions that everyone should have answers for, for we never know when the time may come in our own generation when we will experience war, and, because man's natural, impenitent nature will never change, wars after wars will be with us in the world until the end of time, as all of history including recent times has shown to be true, and as Jesus predicted.

"Where do wars and fights come from among you? Do they not come from your desires for pleasure that war in your members?" - James 4:1.

Wars are cataclysms of nations. All wars and disputes come from the corruption of man's heart. If man were pure in heart, he would strive for nothing but peace; but wars occur, and we need to know how to deal with them.

Many Christians believe that war should be avoided at any cost. Others believe that participation in war should only be undertaken when all efforts to resolve the issue by peaceful means have been exhausted. Most Christians are pacifists and opt for neutrality. They believe that war is never justified or condoned in the eyes of God, for worldly mindedness is enmity to God (James 4:4). However, some Christians believe that war can be justified ethically, as well as their participation in it.

St. Augustine of Hippo and Thomas Aquinas played critical roles in delineating Christian thought regarding what constitutes "just war," and about how Christian teachings of peace can be reconciled with participation in war under certain conditions.[112][113] Their concepts have affected how Christians think about war ever since.

<u>Just War</u>

Strictly speaking, the so-called just war theory applies only to nations (states), not to individuals, although an individual can use it to help them decide whether it is morally defensible for them to participate in war. It acknowledges war as part of man's nature, something which is not likely to change. The international rules of warfare are based on this theory, and they form the legal precedents for charging abusers with war crimes.

The just war theory was revitalized in the 20th century to cover the nuclear era, and then in this century after the terrorist attacks on the US on 9/11/2001.[114]

Some of the conditions for just war (jus ad bellum) are as follows:[115]

- A just cause for fighting must exist (e.g., self-defense against an invasion, versus to acquire wealth or power).

- War must be declared by a nation or ruler.

---

[112] https.//www.gesnc.com/cms/lib/NC01910393/centricity/domain/18/just-war%.
[113] https://iep.utm.edu/justwar/.
[114] Ibid.
[115] https://www.bbc.co.uk/bitesize/guides/zbygjxs/revision/5.

- Reconciliation must be sought before war is declared.

- The aim of fighting should be to promote and perpetuate good, not evil, and with the objective of restoring peace after the war.

Our Lord showed righteous anger when He made a whip of cords and drove out the sheep and oxen from the temple, and then when He poured out the money and overturned the tables of the money changers (John 2:15).[116]

It appears that, under certain circumstances, Christians and churches have a choice between renouncing violence and refraining from participating in war, and fighting or otherwise participating for what one believes is right and best for his or her country and the world.

It is something that is left up to the individual's conscience. It depends on the answer received after earnest prayer to God for His direction and guidance regarding the matter. It depends on how we feel, how we come to grips with the forces of good and evil, compassion and pride and charity and selfishness that dwell within us. If we cannot go forward, then we must abstain from participating. If we can go forward, then we are free to participate. It is a Christian responsibility that must be faced whenever we find ourselves in such a situation. As we will see, it does not appear to be a black and white issue. No one to my knowledge ever said that living a Christian life would be easy.

What actually moves a Christian man or woman in their spirit to take the bugle call to action – what convinces him or her to take action – is uncertain, but it does happen. History is replete with examples of where Christian courage triumphed during times of

---

116 Note, however, that He did not drive out the people or harm them.

war and imminent war. No better example can be provided than that of the American Revolution.

The American Revolution

The signers of the Declaration of Independence, the document that molded the thirteen independent American colonies into the United States of America and led to the subsequent establishment of a unique national Constitution, knew that signing meant their death warrant by hanging. They also knew it meant the sure confiscation of their properties and the ruin of their businesses.

Thomas Jefferson of Virginia, one of the signers, said that it was a bold and doubtful election we had to make to our country.

Benjamin Harrison, also of Virginia, who was six-feet-four and weighed 240 lbs, said in front of the assembly as he turned to the short and slender Elbridge Gerry of Massachusetts, "When the hanging scene comes to be exhibited, I shall have all the advantage over you. It will be over with me in a minute, but you will be kicking in the air an hour after I am gone."[117]

The signers were men who were driven by the Biblical precepts of justice, righteousness and the inalienable rights of man. They believed in free speech, freedom of religion and freedom of assembly, together with due process of law, including trial by jury. The same signers also developed the national Constitution.

Almost all of the signers were Christians, not only in form but in deeds, and all were men of action who were convinced it was time to deliver their country from Great Britain, that mighty tyrant, and

---

[117] Marilyn Boyer, For You They Signed, The Spiritual Heritage of Those Who Shaped Our Nation.

that God had preordained the circumstances that led up to their signing.[118]

Their Christian precepts had been given to them by Britain, but it was a monarchy that suppressed their rights and replaced them with servitude. It was a monarchy that believed that might makes right which, when consistently practiced as it was in this case, leads to oppression, and it had failed to live up to its precepts.

Nevertheless, there existed a dichotomy of views about the mother country. Many were for a reconciliation of offenses and others were for complete independence from her. Most of the colonists were loyalists who, like John Adams, supported the Crown before the imposition of the Intolerable Acts of humiliation that followed.

The Bible teaches that we should fear God, honor the king (1 Pet. 2:17, 1 Tim. 2:1-2) and be subject to the governing authorities (Rom. 13:1). These teachings, if taken alone, without any consideration for the other teachings of the Bible, can cause us to conclude that we have no other choice as Christians but to cower and submit to the demands of an oppressive governing authority.

The repeated attempts by the colonists at reconciliation with Britain through proper petitions and other forms of redress did not result in the least inclination of the Crown to compromise. Most of them were simply ignored or left unanswered. The British only wanted their laws and their word to be obeyed. Coming events cast their shadows before.

As Thomas Paine stated in *Common Sense*, "Everything that is right or natural pleads for separation. Even the distance in

---

[118] Ibid.

243

which the Almighty hath placed England and America is a strong and natural proof that the authority of the one over the other was never the sign of Heaven."

Paine added:

"Europe, and not England, is the parent country of America. The new world hath been the asylum for the persecuted lovers of civil and religious liberty from every part of Europe. Here they have fled, not from the tender embraces of the mother, but from the cruelty of the monster." - Thomas Paine, *Common Sense*.

He further stated that while it may make sense for a small island to rule another small island, it made no sense for a small island to rule a continent.

The four Coercive Acts (the Boston Port Act, the Massachusetts Government Act, the Administration of Justice Act, and the Quartering Act), passed by British Parliament in 1774, which were called the Intolerable Acts by the American colonists; together with the British refusal to compromise; the takeover of Boston before the signing of the Declaration of Independence followed by the takeover of Long Island, New York after the signing; the inhuman treatment of prisoners who were sealed in the hulls of ships and left to die of disease and starvation (after which the ships were set afire);[119] the lust and brutality of the British soldiers who were given free rein to sexually abuse girls of all ages and married women; together with the other barbarous acts committed by the troops against the populace and the properties, crops, forests, trees, and land of the owners who signed; all of these things and

---

[119] The king had proclaimed that all traitors were to be treated as cockroaches that must be exterminated. Ref. Marilyn Boyer, For You They Signed, The Spiritual Heritage of Those Who Shaped Our Nation.

more strengthened the resolve of the Continental Congress in Philadelphia to wage war against Britain, believing that Providence had allowed these things to occur as a great test of their will and resourcefulness.[120]

Again, as stated previously, "Never can true reconciliation grow where wounds of deadly hate have pierced so deep." - John Milton, *Paradise Lost.* Also:

"There are injuries which nature cannot forgive; she would cease to be nature if she did." - Thomas Paine, *Common Sense.*

John Adams, second President of the United States after George Washington, and signer of the Declaration of Independence from Massachusetts, said:

"Lack of action by the people has always prompted princes and nobles of the earth, by every species of fraud and violence, to shake off all the limitations of their power."[121]

On March 23, 1775, at St. John's Church in Richmond, Virginia, Patrick Henry delivered his famous speech:

"Gentlemen may cry, 'Peace, Peace,' but there is no peace. The war is actually begun! The next gale that sweeps from the north will bring to our ears the clash of resounding arms! Our brethren are already in the field! Why stand we here idle? …Is life so dear, or peace so sweet, as to be purchased at the price of chains and slavery? Forbid it, Almighty God! I know not what course others may take; but as for me, give me liberty, or give me death!"[122]

---

[120] Ibid.

[121] Ibid.

[122] https://www.historicstjohnschurch.org/the-speech.

The day before his speech, but yet unknown to the colonists, the British Parliament had passed the "Stamp Act" to help pay for British troops stationed in America during the Seven Years' War. It imposed on the colonists a tax represented by a stamp, to be paid in British sterling rather than colonial currency, on every piece of paper they used. It was imposed without the approval of the colonial legislatures.

What followed were protestations by many who were later appointed by their legislatures to the Continental Congress and who became signers of the Declaration of Independence.

Richard Henry Lee, a signer from Virginia, said:

"Admitting the probable calculations to be against us, we are assured in holy writ that the race is not to the swift, nor the battle to the strong, and if the language of genius may be added to that of inspiration, I will say with our immortal bard [Shakespeare]:

"Thrice is he armed that hath his quarrel just, and he but naked, though locked up in steel, whose conscience with injustice is corrupted."[123]

The result of these things was the American Revolution, which ended in producing the freest, most productive society ever seen on earth, and the best form of government the world has ever known.

Despite the inhumanity done to Americans by the British, Washington ordered humane treatment of British prisoners.

---

[123] Marilyn Boyer, For You They Signed, The Spiritual Heritage of Those Who Shaped Our Nation.

In 1777 two battles galvanized colonial support for the independence movement: Bennington and Saratoga. At Bennington, a militia force defeated detachments of General John Burgoyne's army with heavy casualties, reducing his army by 1,000 men, and causing the Native American supporters to largely abandon the British army. The defeat deprived the British of much-needed supplies, such as mounts for the cavalry regiments, draft animals and provisions, all factors that contributed to Burgoyne's eventual defeat at Saratoga a month later. The victory at Saratoga played a key role in bringing France into the war on the American Colonists' side.[124]

The war lasted for over eight years (April 19, 1775 to September 3, 1783). Cornwallis surrendered to Washington on October 19, 1781, but it wasn't until two years later that the government of King George acknowledged the defeat, all the while keeping elements of their army and navy in America, which Americans regarded as threats, and all the while attempting to negotiate terms, including keeping thousands of loyalists in America, which Washington flatly refused knowing that it would only lead to another conflict between the two nations at a more convenient time for Britain.[125] It wasn't until the peace accord was signed on September 3, 1783 that the war ended.

John Stark, a Major General in the Continental Army who led his militia regiment at Bunker Hill (1775), Bennington and Saratoga, in a congratulatory letter to George Washington sent in December, 1782 stated:

"No doubt the warlike nations with whom they [the British] are at

---

[124] https://en.wikipedia.org/wiki/Battle_of_Bennington.
[125] Richard V. Polbemus and John F. Polbemus, Stark, The Life and Wars of John Stark, 2014.

variance, stimulated by your noble example, will give them further proofs of their inability to trample on the laws of equity, justice and liberty with impunity."[126]

Regarding the new constitution of the land, Benjamin Franklin, addressing the assembly said,

"We have been assured, Sir, in the Sacred Writings, that except the Lord build the House, they labor in vain that build it."

The American colonialists believed that the new government was the best the world had ever seen, and that it set the example for others to follow. They believed that all men sought the same freedoms and were discontent until they had had them, despite how loyal to a particular form of government they may appear to be. Other nations in fact watched closely the new American nation to see whether it would last long. Later, the Civil War was the crucible in which that proposition was tested. Today, most of the nations of the world have some form of democracy.[127]

However, the signers of the Declaration of Independence would be dismayed at how things have turned out for this nation. America today is not as free as it was originally intended to be. The US is ranked 25th of all the nations of the world in political rights and civil liberties.[128] [129] [130] It seems that there now a law for practically everything.

---

[126] Ibid.

[127] According to a March 25, 2022 web article, the citizens of Britain are currently "moving on" and plan to attain their true ambition to be more independent.

128 https://thefulcrum.us/freedom-house-2645382194.

[129] https://www.carolinajournal.com/news-article/freedom-u-s-dips-to-record-low-in-global-rankings/.

[130] The ranking criteria include the freedom of speech, religion, individual of

Returning now to the discussion of the dilemma Christians face during times of war, we must pose the question, should Christians fight against cruelty and oppression wherever it is found? The issue has puzzled many over the years and has confounded the best scholars and thinkers, for the question is unsettled in the Bible, and can only be answered legitimately by factoring in many considerations.

The Word of God has been a beacon of warning to all nations that there will be wars and rumors of wars until the end of time. Do these things not clearly indicate the need for nations to be prepared for war? Do they not imply that freedom and liberty are not guaranteed to any nation that is not willing to defend itself from others?

Many American colonists believed that there were times when the only way to overcome injustice and defend the sanctity of life was by taking up arms. There are verses in the Bible that seem to support and even promote such action, as the following examples indicate.

Verses that Support War

"The Lord is a man of war." - Ex. 15:3.

"Correct oppression; bring justice to the fatherless, and plead the widow's cause." - Isa. 1:17.

"And in your steadfast love you will cut off my enemies, and you

---

economic choice, association, the freedom of assembly, freedom of movement, and women's rights.

will destroy all the adversaries of my soul, for I am your servant." - Ps. 143:12 (a Psalm of David).

"Who rises up for me against the wicked? Who stands up for me against evildoers?" - Ps. 94:16.

"Give justice to the weak and the fatherless; maintain the right of the afflicted and the destitute." - Ps. 82:3.

"Do I not hate them, O Lord, who hate You? And do I not loathe those who rise up against You? I hate them with perfect hatred; I count them my enemies." - Ps. 139:21-22 (a Psalm of David).

"Let the saints be joyful in glory; let them sing aloud on their beds. Let the high praises of God be in their mouth, and a two-edged sword in their hand, to execute vengeance on the nations, and punishments on the peoples; to bind their kings with chains, and their nobles with fetters of iron; to execute on them the written judgment – this honor have all His saints." - Ps. 149:5-9.

"When I bring the sword upon a land, and the people of the land take a man from their territory and make him their watchman, when he sees the sword coming upon the land, if he blows the trumpet and warns the people, then whoever hears the sound of the trumpet and does not take warning, if the sword comes and takes him away, his blood shall be on his own head. He heard the sound of the trumpet, but did not take warning; his blood shall be upon himself. But he who takes warning will save his life. But if the watchman sees the sword coming and does not blow the trumpet, and the people are not warned, and the sword comes and takes any person from among them, he is taken away in his iniquity; but his blood I will require at the watchman's hand." - Ez. 33:2-6.

David, who God said was a man after His own heart (Acts 13:21-23, 1 Sam. 13:14), fought and killed Goliath, and also fought battles with sword and shield for most of his life.

Just before his arrest, Jesus told his disciples:

"And let him who has no sword sell his mantle and buy one." - Luke 22:36.

The verse clearly suggests that Jesus accepted the right to be able to defend oneself.

Nevertheless, other passages of Scripture exhort man to abstain from war.

Verses that are Against War

"Thou shalt not kill." - Ex. 20:13.

"Do not say, "I will repay evil." Wait for the Lord, and He will deliver you." - Prov. 20:22.

"If your enemy is hungry, give him bread to eat, and if he is thirsty, give him water to drink." - Prov. 25:21.

"Vengeance is Mine, I will repay." - Deut. 32:35, Rom. 12:19.

"But I tell you, love your enemies and pray for those who persecute you, that you may be children of your Father in heaven. He causes his sun to rise on the evil and the good, and sends rain on the righteous and the unrighteous. If you love those who love you, what reward will you get? Are not even the tax collectors doing that? And if you greet only your own people, what are you doing more than others? Do not even pagans do that? Be perfect, therefore, as your heavenly Father is perfect." - Matt. 5:44-48.

Jesus told his disciples:

If anyone strikes you on the right cheek, turn to him the other also." (Matt. 5:39), and:

"Blessed are the peacemakers, for they will be called children of God." - Matt. 5:9.

"For God did not appoint us for wrath." - 1 Thess. 5:9.

"Pursue peace with all people, and holiness, without which no one will see the Lord." - Heb. 12:14.

If we stick only to these against-war verses, we must conclude that the question of whether Christians should participate in war is a straightforward and closed issue. However, when we consider as well the verses that support war, such as those listed above, we are left in a state of indecision.

I'm sure that many saints as well as others of a good conscience or religion other than Christianity have pondered and wrestled with these or similar verses. Having to decide between being a patriotic citizen or a good Christian can be a terribly troublesome thing, for the soul struggles for the right answer and has no rest until it is concluded.

In the American colonies prior to the Revolutionary War, the colonists did their Christian duty by first seeking reconciliation with Britain for the harsh and unjust punitive proclamations and edicts issued by both Parliament and the Crown against the colonies.

But when that failed, they had to use other criteria to determine what should be done.

Prior to the Revolutionary War, the colonialists had to wrestle similarly over what to do about the repeated Indian attacks on their settlements that destroyed their homes and tortured their men, women and children to death because it was their way.[131] Should they avenge themselves on the murderous heathens, should they seek a settlement, or should they try to convert them to Christianity? After trying the latter two approaches for many years, they came to the conclusion that the only way to deal with them was through taking up arms. For a nation exists not alone in terms of maps and boundaries, but in the hearts of men.

God gave to the American colonists, as He gives to us, the power of reason, logic and commonsense, and the ability to solve problems, both independently and together with each other, which, with the knowledge of right and wrong that comes from the Bible, we are expected to use to solve the problems of life. During the past two thousand years, a firm conviction in the validity of this truth has produced some of the finest minds and given us great and renown accounts of their decisions and testimonies that can help us decide what course we should pursue in times of trouble.

We're taught in the Bible not only the precepts of right and wrong and the principles of Christianity, but the important precept that the struggle between good and evil, between Christianity and the forces of evil, will never end, and that the dream of an all-Christian world will never be realized.

Abraham Lincoln said:

---

[131] Time-Life Books, Realm of the Iroquois.

"It is the eternal struggle between these two principles – right and wrong – throughout the world. They are the two principles that have stood face to face from the beginning of time; and will ever continue to struggle. The one is the common right of humanity, and the other the divine right of kings. It is the same principle in whatever shape it develops itself. It is the same spirit that says, "You toil and work and earn bread, and I'll eat it." No matter in what shape it comes, whether from the mouth of a king who seeks to bestride the people of his own nation and live by the fruits of their labor, or from one race of men as an apology for enslaving another race, it is the same tyrannical principle."[132]

Ungodly council often neglects other considerations, and advises that it is wrong to let offenses dictate our actions, and that we must not fight against evil or yield to temptations to judge others or cause them harm, and, also, that it is wrong to kill, even in times of war. But God says that we are already in a battle, that our struggle is not against flesh and blood, but against the rulers of the darkness of this age, against the powers and spiritual forces of wickedness in the heavenly places (Eph. 6:12). In other words, we are battling against evil in any case, whether we realize it or not, with the distinction that we are not to give in to rash decisions or shed man's blood.

A reconsideration of things is the inevitable consequence of war that approaches one's doorsteps. It is then that a decision is required. If it ever happens to you, then all available counsel should be sought. You should carefully and prayerfully consider what should be done, weighing the principles and precepts of the Bible against the consequences of the reality of war. Weigh them against the temptation to be part of something larger than yourself

---

[132] Spoken during the last debate between Senator Stephen A. Douglas and Abraham Lincoln at Alton in 1858.

and the exhilaration of the prospect of being able to change your life.

Consider too how would you feel if your home were burned, your property destroyed, your wife and children made destitute of a bed to lie on or bread to live on. Imagine how would you feel if you lost a parent or a child to the ravages of war and found yourself a ruined and wretched survivor. If you have not considered such as these, then are you not a judge of those who experience such things? Are you not also a judge of those who rush off to war to try to prevent such things from happening to them and their loved ones?

WWI, the Russian Revolution and WWII revealed what happens when the antithesis of Christian principles is put into practice. Instead of mercy, ruthlessness. Instead of love for our fellowman, hate for our fellowman. Instead of justice, injustice, oppression, repression and genocide. The juxtapositions await God's judgment on this world, but God allows a nation to come to their own decision on whether or not to oppose such evil with arms, and, as we have seen in this book, He has often used the armies of man as the instruments of His will. He allows man, and actually expects him, to know the Scriptures and to rightly divide them (2 Tim. 2:15), to come to a right understanding of what should be done.

Worry for our posterity often calls many to arms or serve in war in some other capacity that would not normally be pursued. The conviction that they must act for the people of the future often makes the decision.

It is against our new nature to inflict harm or violence on others, but if peace cannot be secured at any price other than by giving in to what is not right and having to live with it, or, if unjust, cruel and depraved treatment of others continues and the fundamentals of human liberties are persistently violated with no remedy in sight other than violence, then it seems that we must take proper steps to stop it. That is not to say that we should glory in the prospect of war, be like mercenary soldiers or soldiers of fortune. But can men and women of moral standing really sit back and do nothing but pray during times of belligerence?

"Man is humbled, and each one is brought low, and the eyes of the haughty are brought low. But the Lord of hosts is exalted in justice, and the Holy God shows himself holy in righteousness." - Isa. 5:15-16.

"Woe to those who call evil good and good evil, who put darkness for light and light for darkness." - Isa. 5:20.

There is something in us that cannot tolerate injustice or unrighteousness. We can never right all the wrongs of the world, as we can never right all the wrongs about ourselves, because there are just too many, but we can act according to our understanding of the Bible and right some of them.

Alvin York was a fundamentalist Christian. He was drafted during WWI into the infantry, but claimed conscientious objector. His pastor, Pastor Pile, even sent a letter to President Wilson to have him excused from active duty. Later, after considering all things, and reportedly after praying for two days and nights to God for guidance on top of a mountain, he received his assurance.

"I received it [his assurance] from God that it were all right, that I would go and that I would come back unharmed." - Alvin C. York.[133]

---

[133] Alvin C. York, <u>Sargent York, His Own Life Story and War Diary</u>.

As stated in his referenced biography, it was the passage in Ezekiel (Ez. 33:2-6) about the watchman, previously quoted, that put a new angle on his thoughts about Christians going to war, and changed his reluctance to a willingness to defend his country.

So he consented and went with his battalion to France in the summer of 1918. The battalion finally got into battle in September. On October 8, in the Argonne Forest, his regiment was tied down by heavy machine gun fire and he was ordered to take a platoon and encircle the enemy from behind. In his own account of the fierce battle in which he singlehandedly killed at least 25 enemy soldiers, silenced 30 German machine guns and captured 132 prisoners, he states:

"Two men on both sides of me and two others right behind me were killed, and I hadn't been touched. I tried to figure it out how it come that everybody around me who was exposed done got picked off or wounded and that I alone come out unharmed. I have been trying to figure it out ever since. Men were killed on both sides of me and all around me and I was the biggest and the most exposed of all. Just think of them thirty machine guns each firing over six hundred shots a minute raining fire on us at a pointblank range of only twenty-five yards and all of them-there rifles and pistols besides, and bringing in one hundred and thirty-two prisoners. I have got only one explanation to offer, and only one: without the help of God I jes couldn't have done it." - Alvin C. York.

For his actions, he won the Congressional Medal of Honor, the French Croix de Guerre with palms, the Médaille Militaire, the Italian War Cross and many other accolades. But despite his worldwide fame and recognition, he never felt important. He simply would say, "I only did my duty to God and to my country, and every man should do his."[134]

Success depends not so much on what we choose not to do, but what we choose to do. Those who risk their lives during times of war thinking about others and giving little thought to themselves are like Jesus.

The closest I ever came to participating in war was in 1969. The Vietnam War at that time was in full swing, at least as was permitted by the US Congress. Being enrolled in college automatically gave me a II-S deferment from induction into military service. Normally, the deferment would have ended when I graduated. However, that was changed by the Selective Service System Draft Lottery held on December 1, 1969. Once the Lottery had been announced, a college deferment was good only until the date of the lottery. Then your chances of entering into military service were dependent on the results of the lottery.

I received a high number, 345. My local draft board ended up taking all numbers under 211. I was not drafted. Al Gore got 30 (Gore then went to Vietnam). Bill Clinton got 311, George W. Bush got 327, Donald Trump got 356, just to name a few high-profile individuals. Nevertheless, I thought a lot about enlisting and even visited two recruiting offices at college.

As in times of suffering, when faced with indecision, it is best to lay everything out before Him. Earnestly ask Him for the wisdom and direction on how to proceed, and you will get an answer. But be careful how the request is phrased. It should be a simple but exact statement of what you want God to do for you. If it is misworded, it may come true only to your dismay.

---

[134] Ibid.

If you pray for the direction, or the steps to take, which will gain victory over the issue, it may well be answered in the way you wish. Nevertheless, the Lord sometimes works in mysterious ways in order to test our faith, which he prizes more than our relief from trouble or suffering.

"The Lord worketh in marvelous ways,
   His wonders to perform."[135]

We need to make sharp distinctions and note carefully how things are trending in the world. This is particularly true during times of war. We need God's wisdom to do it, for our wisdom is not sufficient.

"If any of you lacks wisdom, let him ask of God, who gives to all liberally and without reproach, and it will be given to him. But let him ask in faith, with no doubting, for he who doubts is like a wave of the sea driven and tossed by the wind. For let not that man suppose that he will receive anything from the Lord; he is a double-minded man, unstable in all his ways." - James 1:5-8.

We are to be prepared, but we are also to be confident that we are proceeding in the right direction.

"Be sure you're right, then go ahead." - Davy Crockett.

During such times it is also good to read the accounts of great men and women of the past who have had great trials of conscience but resolved them in some way. When they come to mind, read about them. The inspiration that great personages of the past can provide in times of uncertainty cannot be discounted.

---

[135] The beginning of the Christian hymn entitled, Conflict: Light Shining out of Darkness, written by William Cowper and John Newton in 1773.

As inspiring as the Word of God can be, so great men and women can inspire us to make the right decisions.

The admonition that former Prime Minister Winston Churchill gave to the students of Harrow School in 1941 provides an example of the inspiration that is often wanting, telling us that persistence will eventually produce the desired result:

"Surely from this period of ten months, this is the lesson: never give in, never give in, never, never, never, never – in nothing, great or small, large or petty – never give in except to convictions of honor and good sense."

Churchill also said:

"It is not enough that we do our best; sometimes we must do what is required."

William Ellery Channing said:

"Difficulties are meant to rouse, not discourage. The human spirit is to grow strong by conflict."[136]

C. S. Lewis said, "We live in enemy occupied territory."[137]

Should we fight against the enemies of Christ? It appears that we really have no choice, for our enemies will continue to fight against us, against all who keep the commandments of God and hold fast the testimony of Jesus (Rev. 12:17).

---

[136] https://www.brainyquote.com/authors/william-ellery-channing-quotes.

[137] C. S. Lewis, The Case for Christianity.

In Closing

Dr. Benjamin Rush, a Founding Father of the United States and a signer of the Declaration of Independence said:

"I believe the following propositions should be used as guiding lights in the building of our new nation:

1. That Christianity is the only true and perfect religion; and that in proportion as mankind adopts its principles and obeys its precepts, it will be wise and happy.

2. That a better knowledge of this religion is to be acquired by reading the Bible than in any other way.

3. That the Bible contains more knowledge necessary to man in his present state than any other book in the world."[138]

Finally, brethren, "Sleep in heavenly sleep."[139]

Adding to the last guiding light, everything we read or devote our time to has an effect on the subconscious mind, which can spawn good dreams or nightmares. Make sure your dreams are good.

---

[138] David Barton, Benjamin Rush: Signer of the Declaration of Independence.
[139] Silent Night.

Bibliography

The following books were the major resources used to write this book.

1. Thomas Merton, <u>New Seeds of Contemplation</u>, 1962.

2. Annie Payson Call, <u>Power Through Repose</u>, 1905.

3. Charles Spurgeon, <u>Beside Still Waters</u>, 1999.

4. The Cloud of Unknowing, edited by James Walsh, 1981.

5. Matthew Henry, <u>Matthew Henry's Commentary, In One Volume</u>, Zondervan, 1961.

6. Mark Foley, <u>The Ascent of Mount Carmel, 2013</u>.

7. Mark Foley, <u>The Dark Night</u>, 2019.

8. David Barton, <u>Benjamin Rush: Signer of the Declaration of Independence,</u> 2008.

9. John Witherspoon, <u>The Dominion of Providence Over the Passions of Men,</u> 1776.

10. E. W. Bullinger, <u>The Foundations of Dispensational Truth</u>, 2017.

14. E. W. Bullinger, <u>Cloud of Witnesses</u>, 2017.

15. John Gill's <u>Exposition of the Bible,</u>

16. Archibald MacLeish, <u>The Dialogues of Archibald MacLeish and Mark Van Doren</u>, 1964.

17. Aleksandr Solzhenitsyn, <u>The Gulag Archipelago</u>, 1978.

18, Edward Achorn, <u>Every Drop of Blood,</u>

19. John G. Lake, <u>The Complete Collection of His Life Teachings</u>, 1999.

20. William Meninger, OCSO, The Loving Search for God, 1996.

21. Brother Lawrence, The Practice of the Presence of God in Modern English, Translated by Marshall Davis, 2013.

21. B. R. Teicher, For All It Was Worth, 2017.

19. J. Glenn Gray, The Warriors: Reflections on Men in Battle, 1958.

20. John Calvin, The Institutes of the Christian Religion, Vol. I, 1559 (available online in pdf).

21. Time-Life Books, Realm of the Iroquois, 1993.

21. G. Campbell Morgan, D. D., Pulpit Legions, 1997.

22. C. S. Lewis, The Case for Christianity, 1996.

23. Adela Rodgers St. John, Tell No Man, 1967.

24. Billy Graham, Angels, Ringing Assurance that We Are Not Alone, 1995.

25. Lieut. James C. Whittaker, We Thought We Heard the Angels Sing, The Complete Epic Story of the ordeal and Rescue of Those Who Were with Eddie Rickenbacker on the Plane Lost in the Pacific, 1943.

26. Moses Gbenu, Back to Hell, 2003.

cc. T. Colin Campbell, The China Study, 2006.

8. Gordon Cooper, Leap of Faith, 2000.

2. Dr. Michael Greger, How Not To Die, 2015.

3. Jethro Kloss, Back to Eden, 2014.

26. S. H. Shepherd, A Christian Diet, 2019.

27. S.H. Shepherd, The Cure for Arthritis, 2020.

28. S. H. Shepherd, Don't Take the Jab, 2022.

29 S. H. Shepherd, How to Cure High Blood Pressure, 2022.

33. S. H. Shepherd, <u>The Flat Earth Revisited,</u> 2022.

30. Stan Shepherd, <u>Raw Veganism,</u> 2018.

31. Stan Shepherd, <u>Stop Sciatica and Spinal Stenosis,</u> 2019.

32. S.H. Shepherd, <u>How to Completely Get Rid of Hemorrhoids Naturally: A Permanent Cure,</u> 2019.

About the Author

Religious writer, scientist, engineer and Bible scholar, S. H. Shepherd resides in Arizona. Educated in MI, CO and NM, he is 73.

He has been an avid reader of the Holy Bible for most of his life. In his earlier years, he would read it from beginning to end in about 5 months. Of course, that meant reading it many hours a day, but such was his zeal to know the Word of God.

"I believed in its promises and wanted to immerse myself in it. Today, I read it from beginning to end at a slower pace while dwelling on key passages. Each time, however, I receive new insights and new applications of the Word to my life, for there is an infinite amount of wisdom contained in the Bible and we have such limited, finite minds that I do not see how it is possible for a person to reap all of its wisdom in just several readings, or even in 33 readings, and, as we continue to grow in grace, we glean more insights and receive more of its revelations."

It is by the study and application of the Word of God, and by His gracious leading and guiding, that Christians increase their knowledge of the Holy One.

S. H. Shepherd has written other books with the Bible in hand, but his literary work has barely begun. He has much progress to make before he can sleep. As his favorite poet, Robert Frost, said:

"The woods are lovely, dark and deep. But I have promises to keep, and miles to go before I sleep, and miles to go before I sleep."

Index